THE WILDER YEARS

THE WILDER YEARS

Selected poems

DAVID EGGLETON

OTAGO UNIVERSITY PRESS
Te Whare Tā o Te Wānanga o Ōtākou

Published by Otago University Press
Te Whare Tā o Te Wānanga o Ōtākou
533 Castle Street
Dunedin, New Zealand
university.press@otago.ac.nz
www.otago.ac.nz/press

First published 2021
Copyright © David Eggleton
The moral rights of the author have been asserted.

ISBN 978-1-98-859261-9

Published with the assistance of Creative New Zealand

Editor: Anna Hodge
Cover: Nigel Brown, *Inner Truth* (2006–09), acrylic on linen, unstretched canvas: 1680 x 1810mm
Text art: Nigel Brown, pen and ink on paper
Author photo: John Allison

Printed in China through Asia Pacific Offset

CONTENTS

FROM *FAST TALKER* (2006)

FROM *TIME OF THE ICEBERGS* (2010)

FROM *THE CONCH TRUMPET* (2015)

THREE POEMS FROM *SNAP* (2017)

FROM *EDGELAND* (2018)

NEW POEMS (2020)

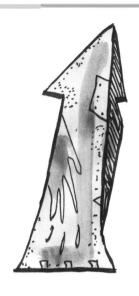

FROM *SOUTH PACIFIC SUNRISE* (1986)

Under Māngere Mountain

The Indian greengrocer smiles,
a Bombay movie star
amongst his deep-red watermelons
orange blistered tangelos
rain-washed sun-kissed mangoes.
Peaches cling together.
Steam rises from the concrete curves of airport motels,
from shower-soaked market gardens.
Cars nose like fish
through the humid air.
The ocean-blue sky unfurls creamy reefs of cloud.
Gentle breezes off the fresh salt spray
sweep across the isthmus.
Leaves are emerald geckos doing acrobatics.
The jelly-green hill quivers.

Big City Rush Hour

Cloud pops out,
a bodybuilder posing.
Heat grills each car on the grid,
bronze light slashes off the windows.
A bus sways forward concertina-style.
A finance house stacks up its cool vertical lines,
calculator-thin.
This town stands as open as an airport lounge.
Everyone looks like a new arrival.

Karangahape Road Celebrates

mango skin jewels Tahitian sunset rose and lime
earth-oven steam, ponga moon, hibiscus sky
a summer frock that floats as she moves
a truckload of drumhead cabbages brakes to a halt
yams, boxes of wriggly pink toes
fat green banana fingers hula their way through slats
in a boarding house Monday stews away in a burnt saucepan
the gullies one long black mid-afternoon yawn
guava hangs on the air, frangipani too like sea-foam lace
cherry stains the purple lamingtons de luxe
through windows and cellophane
an instamatic cheeseburger snaps its garter …

Wings Over Ponsonby

The flat-back ridge, like a Māori workman's outflung arm,
stretches its bulk along to the Bridge and the healing balm
of salt water. On the chunderous Waitematā
the rusty scows growl, and screw the sea into a batter
of white foam, like pus bubbling in a lung,
or like firemen's chemical suds, or draught flagons you unbung.
See there, arum lilies like trumpets blast a benediction
to the thunderous applause of yoghurt trucks winding past,
while the air glitters with gossamer wings made from diesel exhaust
shot out, as if from pressurised cans, by internal combustion.
On the cliff face, schoolgirls bum ciggies from men wrestling up
Jacob's Ladder towards the ghost of Bishop Pompallier,
whose purple cassock floats serenely in the penumbra
of magnolias on the bluff where nuns sometimes do the rhumba.
As the ocean gobbles off Ladies Bay, sour fluid drips
from the overflow pipes of the headland's social mix.
Pom plumbers, prissy potters, dippy models and plum accountants gloat
over pots of dough, an Austin Allegro or horse-race winnings on the tote.
Bulldozers wiggle over torn-down two-storey heaps
to push up a beer baron's blunder of a licensed lounge,
while ejected old maids howl like a junkie botching an injection.
Council blocks are shortly springing up, families squeezing into flats,
like disinfected funeral plots, trimmed and kept by maniacs.
This is what we see if we let our lens go on inspection.
O Ponsonby, harbour of lepers, shop-fronts like raddled lips,
the cross of boarding-house landladies who try to stay respectable,
surrounded by drunks and Pacific Islanders, a daunting spectacle.
Shops stacked with cast-offs, or drapers' slubs, or meat chubs.
Rooming mums with hurting dugs, stentorian, herd weeping bubs;
windy Depression leftovers who are going nuts sniffle, pick up butts
thrown from late-model cars, like gilded tombs flashing by.
Back at the flophouse, one hawks in the washbasin, wants to die.

He has had the filth of living, wants it all to go phut;
through his window he spies a voided coil left by a mutt.
Hydra baulks in large fiery letters into the bland sky;
inside a thousand pigs are razored into slices yards high;
no one keeps hogs here, they are converted by chunks of steel
in machines spinning on grease gobbets in the wheel.
The factory belches the offal smell of beasts in freezers,
up into where the promontory plies its angels and breezes.

The Werewolf of Grafton Gully

I have seen the best minds of my generation
teased by computers,
done up by *Miami Vice* leisurewear
in the wine bar dives of new Ponsonby,
worshipping Art Deco hamburgers enshrined on almighty altars
of junk-food wrappers, rising sons of Samoa's
old running shoes toe-tapping to an unchained melody
of shake, rattle and roll jewellery.
Seen holidays at Ruatōria in a Rastafarian theme park.
All our charismatic Christmases nowadays bearing witness
to rapid rotate rotisserie rock-star corpses
done to a turn by the executive arm of the President
of Random Wipeout Facility Limited
on behalf of United Sugardaddies of America Incorporated.
Give me the massed sun umbrellas of the Waitematā,
the no-obligation mantras of the waves,
as one of the more thrusting big names strides through
the foam sweet foam,
mini-tanker under one arm and a copy of *the bone people*
under the other.
Behind plates of mirror-glass, a written-out write-off does his nut,
goes bananas, cops a case of kūmara, and punches
a recurring rewrite of *This is Your Life* into a word processor,
rising from the crash barrier towards the steel wheels of a vacancy,
in the groovy ruts of the road on the street where I live,
stuck inside a parade of mobile homes,
drunk in charge of a test tube,
with some fish fingers thrust down my throat.
The shops are full of rubber gloves
and suction cups that have lost their suck.
This way to the jumble sales of dirty overcoats, to the shock-horror

billboards dealing in barbed-wire love, on the edge of the very rich
scum, the high tide of human kind,
studied by body-climbing profile shots,
stop-gap cover-ups and lipstick-coated heavyweights,
who watch a lettuce
wilt on video for the McDonald's Murderburger
grubmerchants to the globe,
wired worldwide in Auckland, would-be home
of the Auckland Airport Massacre in B minor.
Behold this landscape of a thousand cocktails,
where sometimes can be seen
the lesser-spotted gum-chewers of Seattle and Chicago,
their Adidas footwear woven out of dollar bills,
each of them pursuing a meaningful relationship
with boogie-woogie,
burlesque queens of yesteryear along for the ride.
Bring on the nuclear-free lunch of Mr Banana Skins
and his transformer robots,
because I have seen this computer-generated generation
stampede the admass barricades of bubblegum,
storm the seven veils of wet Kleenex,
send a Cadillac into orbit, put a man on a life raft,
and build an MX missile factory on Ronnie's Ranch.
Pull up to the bumper, baby, bump it to a trumpet, baby,
take the mainframe to Turkey, baby, culture vultures come closer,
you can wind me up, I'm a clockwork wally,
a walking suspended animation zombie,
a Moriori voodoo dolly,
a living communications network in designer jeans,
heading nowhere in a front-row bucket seat
and one-way mirror shades,
the werewolf on radio howl,
the werewolf of Grafton Gully.
So, get down in the graveyard and dig it, dig it, dig it!

Pictures of Home

Geothermal rock and roll never grows old,
there is a Price Freeze that never grows cold.
A mountain of sheep skulls, supermarkets in chains,
the blue vinyl paddling pool is full of rain.
Hedge trimmer, fruit juicer, a shapely finger,
say cheese, think butter, think milk, think bigger.
A bargain-basement black market,
wool roots anger in the shagpile carpet.
Patchouli clouds, the smell of rubbish also rises,
bleeding fairies in a gone-wrong fairy-tale crisis.
Smorgasbord spread across the Dairy Board,
Anchor Butter autographed by Samuel Butler.
Hacking at the frozen meat,
kākāpō going cheap.
New Zealand, who? Somebody's baby turning blue.
New Zealand, where?
A Social Welfare questionnaire.
New Zealand, where?
The stuffing knocked out of a teddy bear.
On the colour TV in the Lebanese Takeaways,
the Thing is running Round the Bays.

Maungapōhatu 1916

A black Union Jack flutters in the photograph,
their features swim out towards you.
Light gropes along gullies,
Death's Cenotaph awaits the Last Quake.

The Crown held the land and
vapour trails of Empire wreathed
her blue triumphal arch, which dims now
like the glow from autumn leaves.

Sunk in a polished black dawn, the prophet,
when nails ripped from his yawning house,
felt pushing in from the sea the wind,
smashing up off a skating silver sea.

Black mud slicked handcuffed hands;
his hair was a tangled alphabet.
Horse hooves clacked like skulls;
the barbed-wire harp was strung and would sing.

An Otago Gothic Calendar

In January, neighbours seem alien like horror-movie mutants,
in February, hot afternoons crawl through suburbs of anxiety,
in March, slow rise the fumes of Sin Deodorant,
in April, emotional cripples celebrate their deformity,
in May, the Toothpaste Shampoo Queen massacres the Innocent,
in June, all Kiwis advance closer to their Gallipoli,
in July, grindhouse beef is beaten into Edwardian meatballs,
in August, sonic rock implodes in old-time music halls,
in September, a Mosgiel girl wins a holiday to Argyll not Tahiti,
in October, whaler pirates sail past Waikouaiti,
in November, students blunder through the wee garden of Charles Brasch,
in December, the Early Settler's Nemesis waits for it all to go smash.

Eel

A million years fell out of the sky today,
and swam towards the end of the world,
like an old fat eel that knew everything.
It curled with the energy of city,
then went as straight as the empty horizon,
and knocked over a pile of fuel.
It fed on fossils like a black hole
feeding on light.
It fed on the eternal fires of uranium,
as if it couldn't get enough of the burning.
Its heart became a core of molten aluminium
pumped through rustproof tubes which began to burst.
Its tungsten flukes,
hardened in the furnace of a mutagenic brain,
began to shatter.
The turbine blades of its teeth
electrocuted humankind.
Its body broke up like a burnt-out rocket casing.
Its head became a bunker of concrete
eaten by radioactivity
spitting atoms, as disturbed as people,
in the face of all creation,
which began to catch the disease
today at the end of the world.

Painting Mount Taranaki

Mainly I was led to them, the casinos of aluminium,
by the gift of eyebright, whose hollow core contained
a vision of the coast and on it the cone shape,
like a pile of drenched wheat, of Mount Taranaki.
In a world covered in silica and
chucked-up alkathene, fibrolite, aluminium
it is just a peak surrounded on three sides by water.
For the Soviets, holding down a floor
of the Los Angeles Hilton is a forbidden
progression of the open society.
So, to the French, whose own symbol is an ageing Brigitte Bardot,
the mountain, just the same,
could be a logo for the butter they've no-noed,
dismissing a country's living tannery with a sniff:
the hides of rain-slicked cows only acceptable
in the corner of a page by Frank Sargeson.
Corrupt innocence, a young brain, prodded Techtones,
featureless Features, a shot Texan burger bar,
the list is endless but not one story seems complete
on its own, even tying up the numbered dots proves
less efficient than you might at first think
and, anyway, this absurd reductionist format is one
which can only begin to hint at the complex
underlying reality.
Gossamer threads in air, truck belting down the drive,
irresistible wind urging on the silver mist threads
over the split, cheap graves and into green Norfolk pines.
During the Vietnam War Against Imperialist Aggression
I was schooled in classrooms near Māngere International Airport
as venerable millennium temples blew into
millions of fragments in lovely orange and black

negatives—in a variation on a theme
a close study of the status of stainless, chrome, plastic
superheroes revealed wild discrepancies.
Over the various eye-witness accounts
whirred the blades of gunships trailing and corpses
surfed by on an extravaganza of black Coke.
Later, as I put down another batch of jungle juice,
I began to learn that Man cannot live
on home-baked bread and granola alone.
So much up, I moved closer under the mountain
until I stood inside a convention of car dealers
in an Inglewood hotel.
Young and hopelessly flippant, I felt
I should be in an environment where it was easier
to make a buck and people were more understanding
about 'in' references about tribal totems.
I swan-dived through the sex shops of Wellington,
reaching towards vibrators in a glass case, only
to catch onto a picnic papercup then an electrified fence
as it threw the other way
on an elliptical approach towards the majestic
funeral mountain that figures at the violet centre
of the windscreen first dotted before being laced
by the rain caught in the drum-machine motion of Jupiter,
spearing the side of a ponga with a flaming asteroid,
the cosmos being full of Hauhau vistas.
In the snowstorm black-visored Samurai rode on
hornet-yellow Yamahas past a chipped, white,
enamel basin on a window ledge,
a plant trained to crawl up that same window,
the richly decayed caskets of auto wreckers' yards,
the tea kiosks of tourist stops
and up the winter volcano to the extinct lip.

From ash to dove to puce to brandy
the undersea turbines smashed the tints
of the glassy waves into sloppy froth and stiff whites.
A litany of rejects from dye vats,
the unwanted energy of their beauty decorated the feet
of the giant for whom the many Victorian explorers
also left souvenirs.
A string tie, cedarwood fan, lace-edged cambric,
saddlestrap, sherry glass, wristwatch, nightgown, velvet ribbon.
In the centre of ferns they were given back
the ghost images of sedated depressives in the foetal position.
As I scrubcut my way around a backblock wilderness
as unknown as Europe it was I who began to crack not it.
The mountain 'Egmont' rained down its ciphers as I slept
until I entered the psychologically tropic world
of heat and fever, lava village of the last upthrust.
Dealing with the giggling mountain, walking it,
you felt you had seen one of the quadrants,
fundament and crotch scored
between the arched legs of the world.
This province began to experience happenings.
A two-headed calf was born at Stratford,
at Bell Block at evening an old-age pensioner
hung himself by his shoelaces in a Corporation bus,
Dow Chemical Plant mutated into a radioactive centre,
firing out supernovae.
Sacred sites became fictions and sensitised scraps
of computer card in plastic envelopes were irrevocably
drawn into the throbbing whirlpool of events.
A drudge in a hotel kitchen cornered the market
in replicas of credit cards by fabricating a deception
which played on the public's mounting fears of eruption.
His prolific operation soon saw him zooming

to the top of the money tree.
Bizarre mission for a steamy morning, hunting
through the underbelly's growth canopy
for signs of the tribe as showers sweep down
and a rackety V8 is driven from under
a dilapidated carport overhang with the rain seeping in,
the tribe collapsed like a rusty barbed-wire fence
in front of a wedding-cake house with soft pink icing
spelling out blushes and little tears of joy
in the happy hour.
Scrawny wētās skipping across cushions of green moss
on fallen old tōtaras. Neat, eh, to see
ragwort, cocksfoot, fennel, catmint growing
round a shagged dinghy on a rusted cradle trailer
as wraiths ascend supplejack and the beekeeper
is rooted to the spot with a curse.
And now with the art that goes through daily life
the fundamentalist preacher, like a page of old history,
speckled, damp with mildew spots,
his Brylcreemed waffle of hair catching the morning sun,
walks in the foreground of cones of gravel,
central and terminal.
Stained stacks of *Truth* newspaper in the skew-whiff shed
adjacent to the off-balance dunny.
In the wool-shearers' abandoned quarters
a few stained, bloody mattresses, stuffed with kapok,
have burst.
Cherubim perch on the shingle, ice-cream
types of gentlemen swing their partners
like candyfloss in a spin.
A bruised young mother,
with her mother in a trouser suit
and upswept wings of punished hair,

recalls knitting needles of the circle clicking
like train wheels
in the pink-wafer light that reminiscing imposes.
Quattrocento fanatics didn't have it like this.
From them we borrowed cardinal red and pageboy hairstyles,
our larders and pantries stuffed with wholemeal loaves
on the rise, in ferment.
Beans swelling, sprouting out of their jars.
Nuts pouring from plastic sacks.
The stillness leads on into a chapel hush.
Grated carrot bristles.
The dinner guests shrunk
back from the gurgling wine like tarnished coins
thrown into a pocket
the questing forefinger seeks.
A Model-T Ford car hulk planted
in front of the mind like a zombie chariot before the cult of skis.
A battery of children
winding in a crocodile, candles aloft,
their seed teeth bared at the effort of the pilgrimage.
Those ropey arms and flayed legs are not
starved of sensation nor the sharp black/white
as the light snaps on.
Don't knock yourself out,
Taranaki will be there in the morning,
the snow a gunky white blob of brilliantine,
an ornament, a gargoyle for Bat-Stud.
The town hall, pub, gymnasium, and squash court cluster
below, everything we have learnt reduces to a search
for the pyramid they burned down.

At Auckland International Airport

Flying in from Japan, their tiny world,
the jet dances from pole to pole
on the invisible high wire.
The paper lantern of Narita is a postcard,
a wildlife park of hotels,
a jumbo walloping through the bald, white savannah,
a high-jumping gazelle
wrapped in a net of weaving eyelashes,
a stadium screaming now! now!
to the flaming tridents.
A whale balloons out of your brain
and crashes thirty-two floors,
like a glacier hit by an earthquake.
The frail, pink shells of a metropolis
are filling up with sunset.
Customs is a Chinese laundry.
A Samoan Samson pulls in the hibiscus pillars of home.
The cone of the Yankee Clipper
shapes up like the dome of the Holy Father's head.
The sound of it ascending
bombs through the roofs of bungalows
in the flight path.
Fumes float down and enhance
the witness of trees to a petrol wail.

FROM *PEOPLE OF THE LAND* (1988)

Prime Time

The sun loves hot February to death,
girls do the hula till they're out of breath.
Youths on beaches are flinging Frisbees.
Chaps in board shorts strut the Bee's Knees.
A tiara of lights on the Harbour Bridge,
a Cockroach Democracy behind the fridge.

Gross Crazies of the Junkosphere
are doing the backstroke through their beer.
Spiderman dangles from the lampshade,
a plastic goldfish swims in lemonade.
Civilisation smoked down to the filtertip.
Jehovah in a cloudburst would mean abandon ship.
Coronary bypass drunks pilot cannibal cars,
pursuing their own Paradises, Xanadus, Shangri-Las.

God Defend New Zealand

When young men no longer pick the peaches at the beaches,
and the West Coast coal veins have been taken too far;
when the gold and orange dreams leave the crayfish pots,
and supermarkets stop leaking Classical Gas,
                              God defend New Zealand.

When the Golden Gorse hums no more with bees,
and blue heaven's blackberry delights fail to please;
when old ladies brush their hair into atomic clouds,
and Auckland pubs lose their sweating crowds,
                              God defend New Zealand.

When teenage yahoos quit going on the razzle,
and the Tasman Sea gives up its dazzle;
when the cow-nipple of green Taranaki ceases to spout,
and the neon sky-writing of Newmarket goes out,
                              God defend New Zealand.

When Henderson's purple river of wine won't flow,
and the waving wheat carpets of Canterbury don't grow;
when the fruit machine of juicy Nelson breaks down,
and bobby-calf trucks buzz off from one-horse towns,
                              God defend New Zealand.

When the salt lake vanishes from lonesome Marlborough,
and Otago's blooming cherry trees no longer bother;
when Japanese power tools blow up as they shape the land
and kids will not play on the crystal sand,
                              God defend New Zealand.

Talking Cow Cockie Apocalypse Blues

When the Prime Minister gets the sack
and expatriates start coming back,
when letter-writing troglodytes leave their lairs
and exhibitionists keep on their gears,
when the zoos and toilets are full
and the Bank of New Zealand goes bust,
when I win the All Stars Poem Award
and they nuke us into the dust,
when Revelations and Nostradamus come true
and the Big Eye eyeballs the globe,
when the power-hungry have enough
and rubbish dumps turn into gold,
when moralists relax like pigs in clover,
that's when it will all be over.

Just Another Kick

Goggle-box talking head says something clever:
Beyond Pork Palace on the never-never.

A pimple on the face of the earth vanishes forever;
The face in the mirror looks back in terror.

Walk on by with rubber legs, rubber neck too,
But I only have eyes for you.

Stop, stop in the name of love.
That'll be the day; it's not enough.

Echoes from the underground carpark;
Happy days; watch that bright spark.

Fire alarm goes off at the battery farm.
The chook-killer with the chainsaw means no harm, keep calm.

Bright lights, glassy stare, we all live in a fish tank.
I wait at the taxi rank; everybody looks swank.

Bumper to bumper down memory lane.
You are my sunshine; we're singing in the rain.

Lily-white Boy Scouts roll out the red carpet;
If that's your car, Sunshine, you better park it.

This People Person from television land
Says the going form is getting out of hand.

On return of your refundable deposit,
Get a key to the skeleton in the closet.

Out of the closet and up against the wall;
Get up, get out, sock that beach ball.

Throw a ring around the world,
Looking for that certain girl.

It could be you, alone and lonely,
Me your shop-window dummy, the one and only.

A Russian dog jumps over the moon;
A great white shark cruises the Blue Lagoon.

Ice-cold in a Wet Look bathing suit,
a frozen smile, a case of the cutes.

Always game for laughs and walk-on parts,
You leave a galloping epidemic of broken hearts.

Fuzzy bubbles through the champagne spray—
Fun, fun, fun till Daddy takes the car keys away.

One-nil, love-all, twenty-twenty, lucky thirteen;
Sometimes an extra scoop of ice-cream, life is but a dream.

The Last Moa Hunter Leaves the Otago Museum

I saw the Last Moa Hunter fly out of the Museum
on the back of a bumblebee.
Quieter than the suck of milking machines,
more delicate than blind runners on a sponsored jog,
he rode to the golden syrup hills.
The sky was as hard as stale bread,
the sun was sinking like melting butter,
when he leapt onto shell-white clouds,
and pointed out to the cold, pink sea.
Above this old sheep skull of a town
the Last Moa Hunter, throwing a sunbeam,
was hatched into his Apotheosis.

From Our Bush Mansions Facing the Sea

From our bush mansions facing the sea,
bathtub boats, castaway clouds,
crinkled fragments of tinsel,
and a pressure of water reflected
in rippling movements on panes.
Popping sequins, tiger lilies, spotted slippers,
flowering mānuka, hibiscus curls,
all bedraggled, like a blurry dive
into drowning rip tide, the colour of whiskies.
A flux pulses on land back, on leaf rib,
on thrashing fish spine, as
some hawk hovers in the electric crystal.
Wooden webs of rooms and stairs,
fretted sea lace like Edwardian doilies,
barbecue smoke, steamy hāngī weather,
intent kids hotfooting it across sand.
Dank denim of drunk swimmer wading from
ringing sunshine and ultramarine announcements.
Cloistered ridges, ranges and volcanic rims.
Opulent hill breasts nestled in early, voluminous
mist gauze, pockets of lush native bush
stretching fragrant pits across escarpments.
Drops noisily splashing down gullies,
where eels stir from underwater caves
to break the surface in masses of tiny bubbles.
Sweating, spitting, scanning the shiny horizon,
as luminous summer's shallow clarity laps
shell curves, threadbare cotton and frosted beer.
Soporific, armchaired afternoons
on grandfatherly verandahs, half-sunk
in varnished domains, near vanished

in the greenish oil sap essences of sticky stems,
in tasselled toetoe and spangled magnolia.
The evening's dusky fingers peeling away
the thin silky membranes of light,
leaving a dolphin-sleek waterbirth
of blubbering waves, seaweed ravines,
rock spires, dwarf cathedrals, salt basilicas,
pebble-dashed rearing organ pits,
cauldrons boiling long fat strips of kelp,
darkened hit or miss brilliance of starry surf,
sockets of a beached cow skull dribbling foam.

Meditation on Colin McCahon

On the tides sea-sponges sail and weather minor squalls.
Seawater spirals round rock oysters. Everything feels yeasty and lulls
the senses. Raw bloodheat. Raw tar bubbles. Thin frocks.
Deep sunlight ravishes the upland bush and forestry blocks.
See-through hoses snake from the tanker to the tavern.
Trucks bowl past wooden marae with a gasoline alley rhythm.
Grease monkeys clamber round the lube pit at a Caltex stop.
On the open road a long-haired bikie goes over the top.
A demon in his zap car, red light flashing like a strobe,
is in pursuit. Today, water hangs on every leaf-tip like little globes.
Going down in the Indian summer, past a tumbled stone cairn,
feeling mixed up and shook up, I think deeply of Colin McCahon.
My eyes have seen his frail kites, walls of words and frameless banners.
They are pointing cenotaphs heaped with wreaths and funeral honours,
but this hard, spare picture-making is no kind of decoration.
It's a rip: the undertow of vast absent images is the Imagination;
all our other terrible talents by comparison seem to be faking,
his hot blacks and ghostly whites are emblems of universal painting.
Such suggestive power! Emotional locomotives and dynamoes!
In grandeur alone, I consider he rivals the Medici magnificoes.
He can grasp the rumpled skin of a face split by a grin,
capture the wet heat of a storm, explore our uneasy concepts of sin,
show our gold reefs and singing grain of kauri, green volcanoes,
hanging fringes of blubbery leaves, haka in the prows of canoes.
A swirling necklace of seagulls, the arm of the Lord in a gale;
teach us wisdom here on earth, condemn a heritage for sale.
In the galleries, the critics haggle about how to recognise
that what they are really seeing is Adam and Eve expelled from Paradise.
The mob prefers a wanky nude from the school of Coca Cola Pop Art.
Strewth! Slobbering over breast of chicken in the knocking shops of Art!
Skim a stone over a river, brew the billy in a sunless gully.

Far inland, far up a steep hillside on a horse, a cow-cockie
is alone against razorbacks bending over and over away
into the Ureweras. Dream in a dream. A sting in the honey.
Clouds, tiny bubbles of vapour-like milkshakes, froth and burst,
separating and driven before winds in from the coast.
Mushrooms, their damp translucent caps nuzzled by my hands,
sheep's mouths and light, grow in clusters by bowling pavilions.
Old porches, glass verandahs, arches, canvas canopies
seen in the darkening gloom are our Victorian legacies.
In the freezing works, pink and white butchers are stroked by the Phantom
of the Beatific Vision in a robe, holding a kerosene lantern.
Blood and bone, membranes and viscera are pressed
into export slabs. Sides of mutton frozen stiff
go up on slings and spin slowly over graves and hospitals
and public gardens to sink into the holds of ocean-going vessels.
The job of the artist is to provide translations
for everyone's reservoir of half-felt inspirations.
This painter's works celebrate Man's Dramas, Mega-Death,
the sacred mountain, the lake, the gate, and just taking breath.
The noble figures of weeping women wooed by the risen Christ
belong to that part of us for which there isn't any price.
Divinity, Eternity, trying to understand leaves us emotionally drained away,
like lunar planting or mantra chanting. I never thought I'd see the day
when I would come round to believing for my part
that the victory of the spirit goes on climaxing in High Art.

Postcard

Opening a refrigerator,
you find Port Chalmers.
Now and then a little light comes on.
Two bottles of milk are white breasts
in the fists of a milkman.
In the dairy,
a member of the counter-culture grinds the Turkish blend.
A fly reads the fine print on a fishtail.
Rain is a sad lover,
chucking cheap beads onto the cemetery grass.
Sparrows disco dance in the trees above.
The wind vacuums the flash Wool Board carpet of the sea.
Later, the sunlight tenderly bandages a wounded look.

FROM *EMPTY ORCHESTRA* (1995)

Death of the Author

Rumours of the death of the author are greatly exaggerated.
There's time to drive around the writer's block once more,
to revisit sacred inkwells, to download a library of bookends,
to return to sender letterbombs posted by hotshot critics.

In the earnest vowels of the Shaky Isles plots bloom.
A handkerchief scrap of native bush folds into a hip pocket,
clouds twink out mountains, rain crosshatches hills,
waterspouts rise over the sea like twisting signatures.

Novels groan under the weight of their purple prose,
plays are rarefied body chemistry, poems astronomical physics.
Short stories beach on an agent's desk, without purpose,
naming a ballpark figure next to an hourglass one.

A finishing school of novelists, educated to excellence
by a prescription of award judges pronouncing sentences
with distinction, thumbs the edges of a parallel text.
Enlightenment's the glow-worm glimmer of a far-off town.

Static ghostwriters howl in the transmission frequencies.
Reincarnations of Katherine Mansfield, figments of ambition,
write at will, aiming for the pupils of our eyes.
In the Canterbury dustbowl, dust coalesces a society of authors.

Identikit Male

Unpeel from the magazine sample
the latest scratch'n'sniff.
Cordite, hot metal, khaki, sweat:
the smell of Body Bag for Men.
Warehouse warrens of shelves stacked
with bullet-shaped bottles of aftershave:
the man's shaving lotion—Steel Capital.
The chemistry of the elusive god particle
ratchets up the ante to a pheromone frenzy:
graven images of the masculine supremacist.
Issue a summons to the stalker within,
offer a season in the house of correction,
order a paternity suit made to measure,
shut him down, give him his place in the sun.

The Psychopathology of Everyday Life

To be one whose name was writ in icing on a birthday cake,

to be an elaborate baroque curlicue
curving into a marble staircase,
diamanté sunglasses or poolside lounging chair,

to revert to type, to be a stock character, to be a cliché,

to be condemned to the shadows, to a twilight existence,
perpetually reliving the torment of those earlier years,

to be lost in speculation on the Canterbury Plains,

to go into orbit,

to be a flower squashed
by a random footfall in an Edenic garden,

to work loose the wire restraint which is placed
round the head of a champagne bottle preventing
the cork from popping prematurely
in the Bar and Grill

to siphon off excess anxiety through violent exercise
on the squash court,

to be bathed in streaming stadium light,

to believe in the popular mechanics of auguries, haruspications,
palm-readings, horoscopes and water-diviners' wands,

to be a hairsbreadth away from making contact,

to wade into the surf and be knocked over gently
by the tepid swell,

by a lazily sloping shelf of sea,

to swim to the surface as another cloud-capped
wave swings up and makes a kinetic arc,
gliding smoothly towards the beach before toppling
under its own momentum,

to be a rock-like monument, a human alp,

to be like the last of the deep-sea leviathans,

to identify with an elaborate junk sculpture, cameras

boring in, totem poles of slung, splayed monitors

rising from every side—huge, high-definition screens

playing up exaggerated images of body parts: knees as epics,

armpits as marathons, an eye enclosing an ocean,

a shaved hair follicle singing like a kauri tree stump,

to be alone,

to fall silent.

Brave New World Order

Dense bubble packs of freeze-dried philosophy,
seamless natural latex to shield us from latency,
interlaced vines which swing back to LA.

Prisoners of personalised clothing, of conscience, of clarity,
of pastel bimbo chic and pour me a Diet Pepsi.

Deep-freeze warriors scramble for depersonalised lean cuisine,
sent from Montezuma, Valhalla or the Philippines.

Upwardly mobile suicides float face-down in the jacuzzi,
narcoterrorists brainwarped by the firepower of the Uzi,
aerobic airheads going for the burn with reckless audacity.

Fast-track baby computers rubbing out criminals,
men in moonsuits seeking Geiger-counter signals.

Deep black, deep creep, infra-red, rainforest anxiety,
all balanced on the cutting edge of a throwaway society.

Perfect Capital

Apocryphal prophets want the apocalypse yesterday.
Down at the prophet centre, fuzzy logicians field theory,
looking for Einsteinian bloopers in a Powerbook,
electronic homunculus, blinking green brainchild,
a zero, always at the point of no return.
In a lattice, furling and unfurling, time cycles round.
Quick-time smart materials grow up and die;
their embryos shall inherit the capitals, in time.
Virtual particles are short-lived and never seen.
Particular electrons keep away from each other.
An uncertain fingertip slides across a sample surface.
You can never taste the flavour of your antiquark.
One sensor detects body heat; another detects motion.
Triggered by a timer, travelling at breakneck speed,
these keepsake memories I wish to share with you.

The Cloud Forest

In the cloud forest of family trees, with its lineage of millionaires,
dozens of shades of glitter filter down
to the sticky bud of a fern frond,
which is an embryo folded in on itself,
damp brown hairs slicked and combed over into a caul.
It sprouts on the end of a stem, like an Art Nouveau curlicue
in a showroom of Tiffany lamps.
Tribes of glassblowers have lived here, engraving the canopy,
since glass tadpoles first shattered
into Gondwanaland froglets and glacier cocoons were sawn through,
plankton-green, like the interior chrysalis of a capsized iceberg.
Their glassworks blew, moulded and spun pōhutukawa nectar
into bush orchids and puffball fungi,
then into vases, bowls and butter-dishes,
and now into hollow emerald fibre-optic cables,
a telecommunications rainforest,
home of the velvet haunting call of the kōkako,
place of deep satellite footprints, encircled by white rātā vines.
Silica, soda and limestone melt into a glassware
syrup of foliage,
flowing through the jelly fingers of filmy ferns
in the drizzle season marked fragile.
Unlock the engine's valves, seals and plugs
to let the green goo run free.
Atoms in the molecular structure of glass
soon find their way back to crystalline arrangements,
cooling into branches glazed with honeydew,
into trunks buttressed with footnotes left by generations of botanists
opening a green umbrella in search of the tree genome.
A kākā nest-hole buzzes with cellphone squawks,
sunlight coins a collection plate's worth of small change,

a logging camp takes root.
The jewellery remnants of depleted forest histories
are placed in scenic reserves—
a settlers' museum of kahikatea butterboxes,
a florist's shop-window of white kānuka in November.

Takapuna Beach

A radiant glut of water, a marbled ocean,
luminous like the glittering green heart
of a pounamu carving revolving in the mind.

Aotearoa's a dreamboat on a perfect ocean,
the America's Cup's found in a cornflakes packet,
a runabout carousels loudly round a ruffled yacht.

Daylight's ferris wheel turns, the ocean burns,
silky tendrils of surf, all gurgle and fizz,
dry out into sand and scrunched shell.

A bounty of boutiques smelling of ocean,
a breeze is stroking the back of Takapuna Beach
disappearing into the sun's gift-wrap of glare.

Flung up above the rim of the ocean into silence,
the evening moon glows orange like barbecue carbonettes,
the sea goes on writing summer's outline in foam.

I Imagine Wellington as a Delicatessen

I imagine Wellington as a delicatessen visited by Walt Whitman
and Allen Ginsberg, arm in arm like South Pacific sailors.
I imagine Wellington as a delicatessen, and Cook Strait as dancing
a Viennese waltz out of Walt Disney's *Fantasia*.
I imagine Wellington as a delicatessen enjoyed by the grey eminence
of Holyoake in the year of decimalisation, when *Shindig!* dancers
did the Mashed Potato.
The delicatessen's airs are the pointilliste colours of chopped, glazed fruit
in cassata desserts.
The delicatessen's airs are rainbows of steam
above shimmering haystacks of angelhair pasta,
and the lone, stern colossus choosing lunch at the Captain Cook Exotic Salads Bar
is an heroic explorer discovering bell pepper archipelagos,
or a small continent made out of pineapples.
I imagine foodies held gorgonised by Wellington as a delicatessen,
for not only do the pastry coffins of meat pies no longer crack and flake,
maimed to dryness behind warming oven glass,
but the lollipop stoplights stay a sweet, sticky red,
while Milkybar kids in white Stetsons
twirl black lariats and ride out to Kilbirnie
on golden palominos of crumbling hokey-pokey.
If Karori's household spiderwebs are spin-doctored sugar,
and Parliament is a prosy palette of pastel creams;
then the Reserve Bank is all trim noughts of nougat,
and Courtenay Place is a squeaky, icing-sugared, Turkish delight.
The Xmas sponge trifle in every Pyrex dish rises to perfection;
the aroma of coffee, expressed just so, swirls up
to hills crowned by mock-cream clouds.
Lakes of milk and orange juice waterfalls give way
to charred barons of beef,
to charnel catafalques of mutton,

to fanfaronades of boutique beer.
I see scumbled peaks of blue vein cheese rising
over forests of perfumed liquorice, scented vanilla, aromatic bergamot,
over creeks flowing with the bitter-juiced resins of cactus aloe,
over off-shore islands of tart lychee or globular loquat.
Sunlight white as vanilla ice-cream
slides along the clean curved tongue of the coast,
for the delicatessen is a temple of hygiene
lapped by aching green acres of billowing ocean.
I see Te Rauparaha with a bellowing conch, taniwha as Triton,
Olympic warrior on a pearlescent half-shell,
beneath rubescent skies which foam with stars,
like the stellar vintage of a Marlborough winery.
I see Bishop Colenso ascending to Heaven
above the cat-burglar clack of corrugated iron ridges—
free of the tangle of roots, trunks and blind staring shrubs
in every profane shadowy garden,
clear of the sodium auras of the assassinated night.
Tomorrow's Cinemascope dawn will flutter blue,
like slick cellophane Sellotaped by the fingers of the poet
across the gravy stains of fading things.
Tomorrow, the cracked King Edward fonts of the Miramar Palace
shall brim with rainwater in the silence of Armistice Day.
Tomorrow, new Odeons and old pagodas on Oriental Parade
shall be supported by reliefs of African pachyderms,
as a poppy blaze wreathes the charabancs of Manners Street
and Sunderland flying boats, carved from ice, wing it for evermore
over the baked Buicks and cooked Chevrolets of high summer.
The commissionaires of the soft drink concession,
the microwave wizards of the popcorn buckets,
will come into their own,
and the poppadom wafer, the pretzel stick, the halvah biscuit, be held aloft.
A swimming pool split by an earthquake fissure

shall fill with boiling goat's blood,
as cupcake cupids cling to the copper cuspidors of Britannia Old Boys
and Cherry Coke cherubs chortle round Cuban humidors.
Tomorrow promises a fabulous Babylon
of suckling pigs and gelatinous ducklings
in the Wellington I imagine as a delicatessen.
In the Wellington I imagine as a delicatessen,
the capital is a cakescape on a glittering salver,
looped with festival garlands of bottlebrush tinsel.
Its piped icing is a woven tracery of gold threads,
whose vast pattern has an uncertain depth to it,
like reflections in a windowpane,
as translucent as yesteryear's parasols
caught in a sunshower on a Sunday promenade in Island Bay,
and turning the shallow yellow of lemon meringue pie.

Waipounamu: The Lakes District

Hoisting history on his back like a sugar sack,
the swagger strides along greenstone trails
seeking the true identity of the land, its essence,
in the raw rock of geology that mine batteries
hammered into a spectacular gold province.
Hills lift off from the rim of the Pacific,
inland to the mountain backbone rearing straight up.
All night, the crib creeks are humming home,
and drowned towns float in their canvas shrouds.
They are just the ghosts of their original selves,
an emotional investment looted by snowmelt for
schemes to answer the Question of Illumination.
To tap this yearning for a golden age,
singing shepherds held wisps of tussock
which curled like lighted Chinese joss sticks
on the fan-tan tables of sly-grog dens,
frozen in that glacier known as the past.
Dandelion shock troops parachute from October's
cloudscapes; trees peg out sheets of cherry blossom;
thistledown shakes, nods, and sails into summer.
In the forgotten graveyards, hair grows into grass,
while wind sifts the sweet vernal over and over,
like diggers letting dust pour through their fingers.
Worms tunnel through an over-ripe peach,
mummified wasps swing in their spiderweb hammocks
and fast tyres crush the tarseal bubbles far away.
The Kingston Flyer is chuffing like Stephenson's Rocket
through Waihola, Waipahi, Riversdale and Lumsden
on the Great Northern Railway to Wakatipu.
John Turnbull Thomson cut the runholders loose
with a panoramic survey and the confidence of a faithhealer

in the middle of Queen Victoria's Royal Century,
when the boom-time harvest of Celtic place-names
seeded Central like a nouveau-Hibernian dialect
from Balclutha to Gimmerburn to Glendhu Bay.
Leaving behind the drovers' roads of New Munster,
the Colonial Secretary snowboarded on a tea-tray
down all the shingle slides, one by one, and you cannot
singe his beard of bees with smudge-pots anymore.
Princess Alexandra's imperial hymn-book took wing,
gilt-edged pages flapping, for Peninsular & Oriental,
for Clyde of the Indian Mutiny, for the English Civil War,
for the Scottish border towns—Roxburgh and Ettrick.
A gilded cage closed, then it was the whirlybird era
of Jim's Live Deer Recovery, and a long bungy jump,
popping up to Cardrona to sing of gin and raspberry.
Six hours to scale the Remarkables to the eureka
of six ounces some bushwhacked miner never came back for.
Gabriel Read has his memorial cairn and John Graham's
bugle blows a nameless ballad in the balaclava wind,
through Drybread, Sugarpot and Mutton Town Gully;
but the unknown miner, buried by his earthworks,
lays claim to a monument mightier than the pyramids.
Stormdrifts overnight taper off into flurries, until
the snow-peaks at first blush shine like scarlet kākā feathers
laid over white kōtuku feathers, all the way to Aoraki.
Pigeon Bay Saddle's covered with a bridal veil
of flowering mānuka blossom, visually outperforming
a clown troupe of kea birds in an imp grotto,
further into the high country than the neckerchiefed
rough riders who, like cowboys back from the Boer War,
kick the shale loose on the annual sheep station muster,
bringing in the fleece factories to winter over,
one small mob of wethers attaching to another small mob.

The eye of the packhorse has a yolk-sac bulge, dogs
bark and a storm symphony wheels out kettledrum
thunder, celestial strings of golden light,
a sudden brass band of wind instruments with
rain zithering down to tarnish shiny paddocks.
Hail sprinkles hundreds and thousands on carpentered Gothic.
Autumn ends in a burning paperchase of leaves,
and the crackle of thorn bonfires under a white moon.
Lombardy poplars flame out, Douglas firs stay evergreen,
but winter arrives on time in a glitzblitz of powdery snow.
The hoar frost is a Quarztopolis of ice crystals,
turning weeping willows into frozen chandeliers.
Some strung the coils of number-eight wire into fences,
as trail bikes took to the State Highway with a roar,
and the rainshower passed like the plume of the Shotover Jet
over small towns that are hardly seen for hills.
Tarns prickle with bubbles from upland soakage
at the start of Wakatipu on Mounts Humboldt and Forbes,
and under a swing-bridge Beans Burn tumbles lakewards.
Twin Screw Ship *Earnslaw*, where's *Antrim* and *Ben Lomond*?
They won't join you on the Frankton Arm slipway in June or July.
A hawk skydives; a helicopter chunters to a camera feast,
New Year enters on the buckled wheels of a rusty pram,
and the land's tawny from Arrow Basin to Mackenzie Plain,
all silver tussock, golden grass and burning bracken.
Pasture stands four-square to smallgoods, rabbits and dredges,
to the intersection of Lakes Hawea and Wanaka, from where
Nat Chalmers shot the gorge in a flax raft with his guides
after descending Mount Difficulty in flax sandals,
the first Pākehā to see Lake Wakatipu, for which he paid
Reko and Kaikōura a three-legged pot—Te Kohoa!
Wanaka's Roman-sandalled summer holiday season
is hot enough to boil the radiator of a slow Tin Lizzie,

steaming like a tea-billy at a sawmill smoko.
Dried flowerheads rustle against the radiance,
well-upholstered paddocks shrink; beautified paddocks gasp,
at old drought-maker, sap-inhibitor, shriveller-up sun.
Vipers bugloss is the honeyed heart of the hive
and verandah shadows are dark as delphiniums.
The four-fold path of the farmer leads to hot and cold taps,
the meat-safe's a muslin bag, but the kerosene lamp's gone
the way of Aunt Daisy's and Uncle Scrim's voices on the wireless
or goals from The Boot and Pinetree when Rugby took a capital.
Further back, there was the pick and banjo-shovel school,
and before the Otago Mounted Police, came the redoubtable
fists of Wild Bill Fox to tame lode-fever on the Shotover,
when others paid the ferryman to salt a claim with fool's gold
and Roaring Meg with Gentle Annie wore a tartan shawl.
Braids of rivers run dreadlock plaits from a taniwha's
stone head, so his blind eyes spurt waterfalls
and his chest is the sucking valley of a mudslide,
when swollen rivers heave against mountain flanks
and sinkholes laden with silt roar Old Man Flood's here!
He'd ride the whaleboat Molyneux from its tributaries
to the sea, or disgorge the Matau of its spears and hooks,
if they hadn't drained the hydro-electricity, way back.
Rivers rule our lives, gurgling, puddling, dripping,
lapping, spilling, pluvial, plashy from wetlands,
working the lake country like a bit of greenstone,
turning out a tiki of interlocking curves flowing
into Waipounamu, which breathes its green glow,
its luminous opalescence, into deeper ripples of fern.
Its soft parade of twinkles of a summer evening
is the meniscus of ringletted shadows encircling
glittery green chasms, submerged swimming holes,
a place of moon-drenched underwater gardens;

because the lake environs are a home territory
of purple grape froth, trickling a ripe roses scent
and beetroot palate into our salad day memories.
Views of the lake in its many moods: sometimes quiescent,
like a windowpane stippled with rain, behind which
cucumber leafage and swollen twigs revolve, and you
can imagine fridgefuls of rare homebrews,
or spiced-plum brandy, tots doled out to travellers;
sometimes waves snapping fierce enough to whip out
all the tent-pegs in Canvastown, with a wind able
to upturn a wedding marquee's trestle tables tomorrow.
Days of wooden coach wheels bumping out of the Ida Valley
on the Old Dunstan Road in journeys of the pioneers.
Days releasing meteorological balloons into a delicate apricot sky,
in this landscape we invent, as it invents us—
from rock flake and springwater, from a skiff of froth
tumbling over a weir into the afterglow of the Aurora.

FROM *RHYMING PLANET* (2001)

A Walk through Albert Park after an All-Night Party

Like an old magnolia's magnificent candelabrum—
flames of white flowers which gutter and go out—
life goes on without us in particular,
without us in earshot of any prayer breakfast.
All is written, in snatches at odd hours,
and sandwiched into centennials, or dawn parades—
like weather turning from sepia to television.
Even twigs have the hooked forms of alphabets,
and fool's gold pours from sunrise's crucible
into fires of electric remembrance.
The lightening trees comb out old petals
to print them on earth in new fonts.

Bouquet of Dead Flowers

Her body was braille, was scent bottles uncorked,
was the music score her breath hummed;
and beyond us the sun was the giggling Buddha,
robed in saffron, licking his finger
to tear months from the calendar.
The days withdrew from us like acupuncture needles
each morning when we woke up,
and slipped from the bedding seeking the promise
of orange juice you could take from the moment.
We sailed through seas of incense smoke together,
tranced by the gorgeous melodies of Indian-thighed summer,
by the gardens of wild poppies which grew all around us,
in the deserted volcanic quarries of the holiday season.
It seemed then that stereo speakers, always vibrating
their bongo heartbeat, busy bees in the calyx of a flower,
were the hypnotic metal portholes of our ship,
drumming its way through stormy passion.
Spiky juju crystals of the silence between us
were needed to calm that billowing passion,
and the dances we went to at night
only stirred it up, as the whole world duckwalked
with us, or were dirty dogs shaking down,
the brand-new leaves in that summer-of-love tree
fluttering on the breeze of yesterday's sound.

Hundertwasser at Kawakawa

Buried seeds became his kingdom.
A kauri castle, bleeding its resin,
was the amber silence of his tongue,
uprooted to be landlocked fast by grass.
Gold teardrop lakes, encased in glaciers,
dripped him the burning oils of elixirs.
He brushed fragrant orchids sleeping.
He dyed skies grey, then drew the rain-god,
over a magnificent piece of coast drooling.
Inside the eye of brother tuatara,
he saw splintered rainbows of pāua,
and huia flutter from a wealth of ferns.
He bored a hole through rarest earth
to collect core samples of glowing light.
Wearing a necklace of greenest leaves,
he sailed on a tree through night stars.

Teen Angel

Teen angel, boy racer, teen angel, boy racer.

Behind stone shades of hard black glass,
Death the Teen Angel comes looming up fast.

Boo, it's Drivetime down the Great White Way,
batting past suburbs, and Around the Bays.

Got his shotaway smile, got a double-barrelled jaw,
got a souped-up hearse—a flaming ex-police car.

Drunk-driving Death's Head, thousand-metre stare,
from car wreck to car wreck his career careers.

Teen angel, boy racer, teen angel, boy racer.

Branded, shakes a smoke loose from the packet;
to ease his graveyard itch wants to kick the bucket.

Wheelie-spin take-off, then floor it and swerve,
casket snakes writhing from beyond the grave.

Going at a hundred clicks against the clock;
curve sweeping sixty seconds, racing to a stop.

His passengers, we ride the rattle of Death Row,
to vanishing points, to a collection of black holes.

Teen angel, boy racer, teen angel, boy racer.

Manukau Mall Walk

I came out of the Manukau City shopping centre
doing the Manukau Mall Walk—
the shoeshine shuffle, the hotfoot floogie, the baby elephant—
doing the Manukau Mall Walk,
to discover the Great South Road.
So, I said, Great South Road, where you headed?
A hīkoi went past, marching for poetry,
marching to Mercer, Meremere, or the Coromandel.
A platoon of Hussars on horseback went past,
their plumed helmets galloping towards Verdun, towards Papatoetoe.
The Three Graces went past chasing aesthetic pleasure.
The Virgin in a Condom went past (saw you on the TV last night, Madonna),
and I began walking along the Great South Road,
like a train of thought entering a certain state of mind.
As I walked, I recalled the aura of other more earnest eras.
I remembered the sepia photographs of the Colonial Ammunition Company.
I remembered the worm-eaten histories of the bloodstained ground,
under sprig-studded boots and kegs of legs in slanting rain.
I remembered those early explorers who pushed the boundaries out
into ever more mystic territories—
those explorers who navigated the fur and the dust, the tumbling
tumbleweeds, of the vast carpet plains of the empire of the frivolous.
I walked by horse troughs hurriedly filled with cut flowers.
I walked by closets of dark personal secrets.
I walked by gardens where shadowy shrubbery
suddenly gave way to pockets of blazing light.
I walked by the mystery of a bridge wrapped in light,
the spokes of light a sunburst tiara,
beneath which whales swam to a radiant future.
I walked by grain and grape, by bread and wine, by Sunday to Sunday.
Winged yachts were dancing like sandalled Mercury

over the foam on Sunday;
sails burgeoned on the Gulf.
Some of us were elbow-deep in the kitchen sink,
others knee-high in vanishing Auckland,
there where the real yearns to be unreal,
and people are always much worse than you think.
Some were seeking the true identity of the land,
the original pristine quiddity smothered beneath layers
of modern modification. Was it to be found
in geology, or geomorphology, or did it lie
in the very mantle of vegetation, or in the profusion
of microclimates, or was its essence unknowable,
forever modified by the attempts at discovery,
the way an idea once dismissed as useless
one day suddenly gains currency
and moves out into the general population,
both changing and being changed as it goes?
By now I had reached Auckland, jet-lag city
jutting into the sky, town of dark towers,
town of cool waterfalls, deep atriums and skirted walkways,
town of smoothly efficient escalators and rocket fuel filling stations.
Town like a Las Vegas impersonator;
town where locks snick and razors draw blood;
where wristy whizz-kids are able to make timetables tick
and grandfather clocks chime and bong;
where fastidious bouncers obsessively address dress codes
before applying the disdainful cold shoulder.
Town of my birth and branded on the cerebellum.
How amazing that sense of optimism is,
filtering through the ozone of Auckland
to its blue spurs which glitter like a split-open geode.
How amazing that here, where happy endings begin,
at the gateway to a South Pacific Fun Day,

pōhutakawa is flowering scarlet as a maraschino cherry,
scarlet as the fingernails of Elsa Schiaparelli,
scarlet as a bonfire of old books
surrounded by bishops in soutanes sipping sherry.
Bible verses are ascending in blackened flakes,
whirling scraps of ash above Lord Concrete's Domain.
Whatever next, whatever next, as the wind flicks over text;
flicks over characters from God's hotel
condemned by religious intoxication
to the delusion of ongoing happiness before their last merciful release;
flicks over medicine men quivering in their sleep,
doing a little light mall walking to a tune by Henry Mancini.
So, I'm out here, too, on the Great South Road
in this pandemonium under the basilica of stars, under the Hubble,
doing the Manukau Mall Walk—
the shoeshine shuffle, the hotfoot floogie, the baby elephant—
doing the Manukau Mall Walk.

Drift North

In Ōamaru in early spring,
marking the Day of the Dead with a sundial,
you can face the cemetery from any direction,
and still drift north.

You quietly take your place on the bush trek,
to begin at the start of the day,
where a sandwich cutting leads to the road,
for the drift north.

Bus stragglers muster at the terminus,
wool-gatherers wait in line with knitting,
the backpacker's waving single-handed,
on the drift north.

Tusker, an up and under speculator,
comes a gutser in a puggy paddock;
a grubber, a bit of a biff, then a try,
next the drift north.

Shunt to Parnassus, happy as Larry,
lashed to the wheel in a tangle of weather,
doing the ton in a lather of leather,
just the drift north.

In Kaikōura, you take a squizz,
at waka wake or whale spout-fizz,
while the sky dribbles sweet nothings,
a spindrift north.

The earth embracing kith and kin,
nearer by far to what is at a remove,
traces elements of blood and bone,
seeks the drift north.

Lights fail, snow turns to hail, fences run along,
pets scoot, possums cough, pigeons pack a sad;
trees split, angels flit, mountains winch on by:
it's the drift north.

Deep South

Fog forms a wedding shroud in trees,
the spindrift spun is the spendthrift sea's.
Pianissimo, pizzicato, snare-drum skirls,
then a headlong orchestral rush of applause.

The slant-told rain for which they yearned
beads and veils the shiny petals upturned,
seeds silver floodplains James Cook branded,
gleams on rugby field faces waterbomb-stranded.

Full-grown rivers sob stories of sunken dinghies,
of whaleboats bobbing above anchor stones,
of bullock eyeteeth, foxed with leaf mould,
gnashing genealogies of sun-bleached bones.

Water closets slip their moorings, cob cathedrals
buoy up their bells and melt back into hills.
Water's clear grain englobes black cherries,
as stealthy as fingers flogging food in dairies.

Whitewater froths like hydrophobic dogs,
at tourists agog on prayer-mat rafts.
A flax taproot rots in a brain-sponge corner,
sheds grow green, creeks rock with logs.

Rainbows capsize; tractors sink underground.
Buckled into place, cars skid round and round.
Stopbanks fail, a lake loots a drowned town.
Rain drapes all in its pearl-grey bridal gown.

Shed Light

Let the light in, let light in—
kerosene light, ice light, coal light.
Light upwelling,
light dispelling,
sparks of light, jars of light,
dust motes swirling in delight.

Glad the light
that comes through night,
shedding light on inner gloom—
rose light, true light, lamp light:
storm lantern burning bright.

Shack's nail-hole light is slight.
And just a zither of light
runs through the fight
of entangled, wild trees;
just a glimmer of light,
down from tree height,
ticks and tocks,
rocking in the breeze.

Ladder of light that leans upright;
river of light that flows from sight:
you let the light in, let light in—
shed light, river light, earth light;
brilliant light to journey by.

Dutch Mountains

At night I climb in the Dutch mountains,
where everything's sinking under sand.
A complete town takes centuries
to vanish into the Antipodes.
The wind can make the North Sea ripple
and push the vanes of windmills round.

Every Saint Elizabeth's Day,
tulips float in drowned bouquets.
Stained with engine oil and drizzled grey,
waterways heave like mud-wrestlers,
or horizontal mountain climbers
far out at low tide on sea-polders.

When above trees night-time fades,
many bridges, barges, tugs appear.
A cloud-shaft of golden rays
strikes the water table, shiny with rain.
To towns awash in history
smooth hydraulics bring the trains.

Roads, ruled straight, hum
from the compass of the Netherlands,
whose seventeenth-century boats
left the navigator's name of Abel Tasman,
and a relationship between earth and sky
which floated round the world to find us.

Explorers

Sunset, and the six billion names of God
written in drops of blood turn to vapour.
We backpack our poems through the bloody flux.
When mourning becomes electrified, whisper
in God's ear, rehearsing the sound of tinnitus,
until God turns His deaf ear, His blind eye.
We call him God the Fibber, God the Food-faddist,
and on and on, mad, madder, maddest.

Baxter's and Butler's footsteps left footnotes
to the Alps which made Buller's gorge rise.
Archimedes could find his fulcrum there,
and seesaw on mountains into the air.
God's own theodolite swings like a pendulum do,
over ropes of butterfat and cow-hoof glue.
Numbers of angels on heads of rusted pins
bless the sugar-bag dears counting their sins.

Forest taken from swamp cracked, then died.
Creaky wooden rooms became hopeful tombs.
Artful constructivists mustered the energy
to bring down from every mountain-side
avalanches of sheep, whales of wool;
their prize rosette pinned to Muttonfat Hill;
their Lord's Prayer engraved on the whisky grain
of black label lakes by winter's bitter rain.

The Backbone Club twists from its own sapwood
a kauri gum bible open to the Holy Word.
Solstice like a poultice draws vapours from land;
Pegasus the Sheep flies with hawk wings in his back.

Bestiaries of butchered birds float down
deconsecrated rivers to the six o'clock swill of town.
Afternoon tea is gilded golden brown.
Fiordland is turning to the deeper dark.

Out of stanzas of turned sod, farms expand.
There sweats a gun shearer; there puffs
a wilderness backpacker; there's Hillary's Everest.
A heading dog barks up Blindman's Bluff.
The quest for an ulterior motive leads us
nowhere but where we were already going,
slouching to the sheep-dip in clouds of unknowing,
God slipping between lattices of neutrinos.

The A&P Show Centennial

Victorian town, in centennial brown, studies memories
of holy days topping hot, ladled with oodles of heat,
when folk came to canvas a haymaker of a sermon,
and folk came to petition the faraway gaze of the Virgin.

Now axemen's arms carry family-tree stumps side on,
the thousand tics the flesh is heir to gone wrong—
and no one much cares or wants to wait in a queue
for homebrew hooch, bottled lightning from the blue.

The country bumpkin rides his rodeo pumpkin
buckled at the knees, peppercorns make him sneeze.
Spittle runs off a duck's back, cheerleaders barrack,
cumulus is coached into the best performance of the day.

Not rain's lukewarm applause, nor possum claws clatter,
just traction engine stutter and some cow-cocky's patter,
and the tin banjo jangle of number-eight wire,
and the vagrant fragance of roses stuffed in a vase.

Hilltops lift off on a paragliding video's mini-cam;
stay-at-homes bury themselves down in the dumps;
but the media are medium cool, even oafs use their loaf,
in these days of rage and neuroses dark as Loch Ness.

Maps trace holiday trails along hairpin bends
to towns few and far between, where we leftovers,
peeling off singlet after singlet, might mug it up—
our metaphors agricultural, our blurry vision pastoral.

Farms: A Sequence

i.
Grass

Shoulders up to the hills,
the spirit of great-great-grandad slumps
staring at the sun, his stumps
gnawing fat of the land, side of mutton in hand,
the blow-me-down windbreak around his heart
still fit to beat the band.
His squatter's hut became a town centre in the now
metaphysical bush, rational and empirical
inheritance of compulsive methodists—
a story sown in seeds of grass,
and read by generations,
from the concrete tree of the Sky Tower down.

Shearers left nothing growing on the sheep's back—
clumps were pulled out gully by gully;
standing bush went up in smoke,
burnt to a frazzle, cleared like throats
harrumphing catarrh-rah-rah boom-de-ay,
with the rumpty-tumpty rhythm track
of a colonial militia, in full fig, marching past
the rotunda built on Rūaumoko's rolypoly belly
as possums acted the giddy goat.

ii.
Trees

Place is bottled lightning in a shop,
or in a chandelier's glass teardrop,
or in a glow-worm's low-watt grot,
or in street neon's glottal stop—
wow-eh? wow-eh? wow-eh?

Place is the moulded face of a hill,
or lichen like beard on a windowsill,
or the bare spaces that shadows fill,
or ancestors growing old and ill,
or descendants at the reading of a will,
who frown and examine their fingernails
before plunging off down the paper trails
of diary and letter and overdue bill.

Place is the home of family trees—
family trees to wrap round plots of soil,
tree roots to shrivel into umbilical cords,
tree branches to spill bones and skulls;
but even trees are just a spidery scrawl
against the shelf-life of a mountain wall.

Place is a brood perched on power poles:
bellbirds with shadows of gargoyles,
korimako who clutch the power of one,
like an egg, to trill their familiar song.
Place is grandsons who sprawl
in the family tree with laughter;
place is a tree windfall,
gathered up in the lap of a daughter.

iii.

Histories

Taking whole days to get traction on the bracken,
any kind of purchase;
following, say, a stray thread of river—
straggler from the flock of waters—
to a waterfall, straight down a slate showerstall,
and thence to built-in closets of gully,
big as a small country,
a bivouac of travellers made camp in cabbage trees.
At flaxroots level, they learnt to lay down lawn,
and lay lino against scenery so majestic it boggled minds.
Soon, land bulged like sacks of spuds
where, once, kūmara pits had been dug.
The wives of the Women's Division of Federated Farmers
took part in bake-offs.
Tractor parades of southern gentry, South Canterbury
sodbusters in worn-down moleskins, took off.
Stiff-backed Free Kirk Scots
wintered Herefords in puggy paddocks.
The quest for security with no hand-outs
became wind-whipped and salt-scoured
when economic storms famously wept,
and all candles guttered to Heaven.
Many learned to titivate the tablecloth,
tickle the teapot, keep skitebooks hidden;
to fleece lambs, char chops,
eat lashings of strawberry scoff;
to take dead bush from rough block.
Following the *Complete Guide to Home Knitting*,
one with clothes-pegged nose
ran a batch of scones up the flagpole,
or so rural legend goes.

They were not just Kiwi clodhoppers
with dozers and bowsers, bullocks and ballots.
Fences hummed like tuning forks,
and if you dug down for a corked bottle,
you'd find scrawled IOUs for fortune's Lotto.
Outlaws pulled out surveyors' pegs,
or peered hopefully at tea leaves' swirled dregs.
One drooled in sleep over riverhead gold
on an Epsom verandah;
later there were chancers, intelligencers and remembrancers
off to slaughter like truckloads of sheep.
Now is the wailing and gnashing of well-travelled teeth;
though some, less bold,
settle for placid chewing of the cud
on viable lifestyle blocks.

iv.
Relatives and Relations

Rain is hosing down
on the black-singlet bushmen who subdivided a province,
axe-handle by axe-handle:
Messrs Brown, Williams, Morgan and Graham,
Jones, Johnson and Smith,
minding their own beeswax, a century underground.
Their children became golden girls, bronzed blokes,
many axe-handles across,
some a pack of bludgers living high on the hog;
one gone from bobby dazzler to bobby-veal-broke;
one chirping like a box of birds in frock so tight you could flog
a flea across it.
Great-Uncle (Horselips) Harry once rattled the top brass,
a war hero who never stopped a bullet with his name on it.

After, in his black woollen singlet stained with elbow grease,
he gave the fingers to the flaming softies
crowding the Situations Wanted columns,
by just getting on with it, a hard doer 'til his guts went crook.
Great-Uncle Cedric sailed up the eye-smarting Strait, Cook,
the be-all and end-all of his working days,
a harbour pilot whose tug just plugged away.
Cousin Wilson, tall as a pine tree log,
had to be one of the best known jokers around,
jollying along scruffy sheep and whistling up dogs.
Nosebag Johnson—Joe—was a dearly loved early father
of the turf, with his saddles and tarpaulins,
his winning potions and portions—
his neddies and geegees galloping past us.
Great-Aunt Gail, running with the slightly foxed fur brigade,
painted as a very shady lady,
and Bob—a few sheep short—who set an aerial top-dresser loose
on the wrong property.
Uncle Cleavdon, the creative one, who keeps his head warm
in a hand-knitted tea-cosy,
surrounded by his thrown pots' best shots—
his waistband-thumbed potbellied pot crowns the lot.
Relatives and relations: there they go, up the back of the wopwops—
all elbows and bellow,
their audible birdsong unplugged or unplugging—
they gawked at Death warmed up.

V.
The Wedding

In the season of perpetual light rain,
a single layer of fine gauze outlines the shape
of Papatūānuku.
She was a farm girl, smelling of hay and silage.
Her hair was the orange of willows in winter,
and Wayne was her hayseed swain.
In the roaring days and ways of young rouseabouts,
the river shining-buckle of the Bible Belt turning,
they decided they better get married,
with the blessing of Blood-pudding Dad and Butterball Mum.
Such a new-fangled novelty—
they were away laughing in an all-purpose wedding;
putting on a bit of a bash—
after, at the homestead, echoing to summer's busted flush,
and the right-royal colonial adjectives of raw bush-carpentry.
Bloody hell, yes!
Enough grog and tucker carried into the marquees
for an open-necked good time:
the hoop-ra, hoop-ra of 'For she's a jolly good fellow';
lines spun about knickers twisting from here to there,
which branch into vines, sprouting damp ferns,
maidenhair …
knickers and knockers blooming into knickerbockers …
Sturdy puffer-bellies start to big-note,
like a congregation of heading dogs yapping at bleating mobs.
Crockery does a jiggle to fiddle and faddle,
piano-accordion and guitar spar,
dancers whip about—reel, stomp, wheel—
arms linked in whirl.
Grog gropes through a glory-box of Giddays,
blossoms into a fair old do,

and begins to throw its weight around,
both bodgie and widgie.
The farm shrugs off its motley uniform, then,
of toetoe plumes and gorse tassels;
gets up and goes to town in glad rags, in best mocker,
giving a beer mini-tanker the old heave-ho.
Walrus mo' and goatee beard are arguing together,
muttonchop and sideburn jawjaw,
until the wee hours, bleary-eyed in the a.m.,
when the hardee har-har laughers-in-law
feel they've hardly begun to make a dent
in the lexicon of humorous ruderie.
But then Dawn arrives, and they look homeward,
take stock, melt with rue,
unsnag their yarns; trot to paddocks new.

Chairman Miaou

On the windowsill,
he's as still as a shelf-ornament.
Sometimes he waxes skittish;
chirrups, flings about in four-legged ballet.
With visitors he exerts animal magnetism.
He feels the weight and heft of each day,
by testing his fur with his tongue.

Bat-cat, the pasha cat,
plumped amongst sofa cushions,
he rules over house and surroundings.
He's feared by moths with his boxing paws;
but jeered at by birds as he sharpens his claws.
He enjoys cordial relations with Siamese and Persians.

He has got the voice of an elderly rasper,
he's the secret gargler of sandpaper and vinegar.
His noisy rhetoric sounds insane;
he wails like the whistle of a long-distance train.
He caterwauls like musical instruments having a row:
a violin, a trumpet, bagpipes on legs.
Pick him up, the one-cat band: Chairman Miaou.

If Buccleugh Street Could Talk

A plate of stale scones, a drab bag lady,
with the Octagon your centre of gravity,
dowdy Dunedin, capital of the minimal,
you're like East Berlin before the Fall.
City of butterscotch and antique junk sales,
of walks on the transplanted Hibernian strand.
Descendants of people who wove the heather,
now in sherry-gold or flame-blue cardies,
are a dance of pedestrians joined by blood ties
in the neverending carwash that is your weather,
your lowering afternoon that lasts all day.
Sinkhole, bolthole, considered a cold hole,
a Celtic bog, across which drifts piss and vinegar,
the sour old reek of homemade preserves,
of battered shark's guts and thrice-fried chips.
A catchcan catchment of Third World water
through rusted aqueducts, along rotten flues.
Town full of night owls and first-edition-seekers,
town haunted by ghosts of whiskered ancients.
Time-warped necropolis, one big cemetery,
crepuscular as a funeral parlour,
all stasis, all stagnation, Death's waiting room—
a trapped gas bubble, a cloistered agridome.
Your rain-wet *ODTs* are a place of obituaries,
and your floodlit churches film noir settings,
smeared by a dirty squeegee on a stick.
Elderly coupon-carriers, close to flatlining,
drift like autumn leaves towards the supermarket,
as a mountain bike whizzes down York Place.
The low expectations of the chemically altered,
the guitar blues riffs on the rites of failure,

the bored waving to Russians, Hello Sailor!
You're Presbyterian, grey, made of stone,
but your stony façade hides a warm glow.
Like prize bantams from a bantam-weight chook,
you blow out the statistics in the record book.
Your Uriah Heep humility, your dungeon of grunge:
you create these visions within a single compass,
and as shiny four-wheel drives race to the crossroads,
where the traffic lights are forever amber,
and the Town Hall clock bongs hallelujah
Dunedin, just up from mute, inglorious Milton,
is a name to conjure with in the world.

Descent from Mount Aspiring

This is a descent from Mount Aspiring,
this is a descent from all desiring,
from toehold ridges, from quarrels over rocks,
from the crystal bloom of clouded lakes.
This is a descent from soapsuds, whitewash,
Granny Smiths, from Hairdressers and Tobacconists,
from meat safes, and rifles and spades at Gallipoli.
O immobile crag, round which winds swing,
stake out a place for the New Zealandian,
a place for tin medals and moth-balled gold braid,
a place for rain seeping like a brain haemorrhage.
And should the weather never reverse itself,
remember every stone, every twig, every splinter,
remember every broken shape, every broad back.
For, like skin splashed with acid sometime
in the abused past, there's an old ache burning.
You call it the elixir of democracy; you call it
history's exorcism of scapegoats and xenophobia,
you call it seismic bracing, you call it a miracle cure.
But the earth shrugs, the stars titter, and the sun
beats down, beats down; every minute, saviours are born.
Atlas expands his boundaries and you're in clover,
queen of the silver dollar in a dolphin dawn,
rolling so easy into Bill Gates's gated Eden;
New Dollywool, New Bollywood, New Hollyweird.
What could be odder than to be in New Zealand?
So quibble into frivolity on closed-circuit imagery.
Please block the view; let billboards be put in front;
cradle what you crave; lie down under the flight path.
It always happens at the speed of auto-dialling:
you tumble and fall through the pitch-black jetstream,
a dark homecoming to the echo of an angry god.

Seismographs chatter with whiffs of sulphur;
there's a bar-fly jumper doing the Velcro Fly,
clothing all woven out of coagulated grime.
Level the hills with dirty money; email
the smiley emoticon with the flesh-eating grin.
Unravel the clean Waitangi Day tea-towel,
and put the dead Tamagotchi back on the shelf.
With the laying on of many hands may you
manipulate the eugenics of the selfish gene;
may you pardon this, the double de-clutch
of decaffeinated truth shooting past your downside,
sucking up all the air in the room as it goes,
only to prang at last into the flaming drink.
The hum of cogitation round a gaming table
is the jarring rant of people thinking out loud,
the noise of whirlybirds blown inside-out
above lakes' inverted arcadian Alps.
Hot buttered soul-babe, o butterball of mine,
there's a world beyond the wicker bassinet
of wholesomeness where the pub-crawler goes,
and where portfolios fall open in paroxysms of pain.
Let the mourning doves roost in white polystyrene,
as a globe gives birth to Golden Arches;
let the candle-smoke visions of chained lightning
throw a radiant lasso that fingers vainly grasp at;
and let assorted perpetual motion machines
fidget in the starting blocks of accelerated dreams.
This is a descent to umpire a feast for sand-flies;
this is a descent to nothing that you recognise;
this is a descent to taste fame and not to want it,
because it tastes of the sweat of anonymous masses.
A descent from where cow drool hangs on the breeze,
from where the cloud-piercing lode of Mount Aspiring
leaps like the stuck-out tongue of a kapa haka dancer.

Poem for the Unknown Tourist

Greetings!
No stranger land than New Zespri
welcomes you all—
living anachronism,
Victorian antique,
antipodean geyserland,
inflamed appendix,
coathangers bent to shape outlines,
towers of five-cent tuatara reaching to hard-won paradise.

Land pronounced Soup Pea Ham,
(if you mumble it)
land of omnipresent darkness,
land of pods of Family Fun Runners,
land where mutton falls tied to a golden parachute,
falling falling falling,
land where the name Massey hangs on the air like gunsmoke.

As unleaded islands make backcountry overtures,
our hills reverberate to the sound of gallows
built for the end of the golden wether;
reverberate to memorial ovations
for the Lovelock lap of honour;
reverberate to whitebait in the surf
going ballistic at the umpteenth Hadlee hat-trick.

Take our camping grounds as you find them,
the pastoral exposition renovated as novelty toy,
cowsheds cut out of corrugated tin,
corkscrewing rides and water cannon,
paintball war games and lasertronics.

Flock to follow our flocks;
be shutterbugs clustering at scenic windows;
our creeks leak from reservoirs of dammed emotion;
our dreams are landfill in a well-known ocean.

Let an orienteering team
of giggling geisha girls ride tandem mountain bikes
through Cathedral Square;
let foreign language, do-wop, a capella choirs be heard
in shopping centres;
let wide-bodied new arrivals
try new fast automatic toilets,
and knock back noble rot in vineyard after vineyard,
and milk the odd sacred cow,
and be presented with kiwifruit the size of a baby.

May the bungy-jumper yodel breakfast
over the Remarkables;
may the smack of willow on leathered rump
be to your liking;
may our motels be rusted to perfection;
may you not be dismayed when everything within reason
is out of season.

As the old Pacific hand, tattooed and weatherbeaten,
rows you ashore,
as the pre-dawn hush is broken by chainsaw roar,
as you hold yourself back from the zeal of the land,
may we remain evergreen, ever thine, Aotearoa.

Cutlets for King Kūmara

When I go up to the capital as an honorary white man,
I shall play upon a flute whittled from a thighbone,
and recite the bit in the Bible where it says hui after hui
shall ye hold to honour the Native Land Purchase Agreement.
I will fleece feral Drysdales with shears for wool-bales;
lead four-wheel drives up the drive in mud relief;
then wrestle a colonial conundrum into the Commonwealth:
the sage's manifest destiny is to be part of a spirited recipe.
Horiland, my Horiland, 'tis of thee I sing, and Ruapehu too,
a mountain donated then papered over with Statutes of Westminster.
The International Hangi Pit Food Court anglicises Maui's name;
poets throwing voices rehearse pantomimes of Waitangi Day libels;
and there's an argument of theologians behind the boxthorn:
can possums practise nocturnal consciousness-raising
in the Upper Moutere Valley? should bridled moa,
towing harvest carts of marijuana, be breathalysed?
Stoked archives of bees fly away like stray thoughts;
I've left my collection of failed suicide notes to the Turnbull.
As I prepare to write one last anthem for King Kūmara,
the *Truth* is printed in hot Gothic sauce on a tabloid tablecloth.

The Whangamomona Prophecies

A million maggots shall do a haka
on the carcass of a stud bull.
An army of overstatement will stage
a parliamentary coup.
J'acuzzi becomes leader of the Acid Party.
More jawjaw from relentless motormouths
who plug product over and over,
endlessly talkative about the unspeakable.
Crisis managers will write rider clauses
all over their corporate consultancy contracts.
TV news announcers shall have the aerodynamic
looks of late-model cars.
Out of the mouths of babes and suckling pigs
shall come grunts of wisdom.
Treasury will be turned into a museum
of starched doilies and folded napkins.
The dirt poor get to share equal air-time
with the filthy rich,
and all will be driven on by scourge and lash.
Art'll scale yawning heights of Chateau Cardboard;
the upper crust'll blow off Tongariro's top.
Crossdressers in high heels
will charity streetwalk for Meals on Wheels.
Tyre swans by the front gate will catch on;
and a giant possum the size of Te Papa
will be found in remote bush near Whangamomona.

Tūrangawaewae

I left my life, held captive by a dream,
and stood in the middle of the Californian
Spanish Mission Revival beachfront
learning how to build cumulus clouds.
I saw Napier's blue sky pour it on
in the high noon calm of the sabbath,
and become an electro-furnace bolt-on,
whose countrified backwards centrepiece
shone above the tremble of summer's edifice.

Then I trudged the autumn moa-bog,
to honour the Treaty did a handjive dodge,
snapping Hau! Hau! salutes at Britannia—
a majestic barge bearing Victoria,
though hard to tell she was, from sour
bars of soap, black billy tea, rock flour,
all that candlepower burning pure oxygen
of ideas at Grand Theory Hotel, demolished
after Hell's Gate fires of the last earthquake.

A tūī's hesitant song waltzed around
the rainforest silence of bush lawyers,
and love planted flags on icecap pinnacles.
Profiteers through envy and greed careered,
going by feel, their heart muscles pumping.
Rutherford for the atom was still searching,
in a photograph on the milled edge of town.
Tahupōtiki Rātana gave us that winter,
a kūmara, a tiki, a gold watch, a huia feather.

In hand-to-hand combat farmers got closer,
leafing through leaves, rolled ever looser,
until gardens erupted from Vogel's ears,
his beard of spring clematis cut by shears.
As bush began to fill with supermarkets,
as skies began to puddle with vapour trails,
as seas began to poem with stress marks,
I undid the rusty clasps of an old century,
and stared down into my life turned to dark.

Electric Pūhā Telemarketing Ode

Straight up, yes people, we burn like red meat,
hyped to go ape disaster-wise when wired.
Your memories of President Cadillac have been retired,
now that wildcat operators have staked out your seat.
Goodyear inner tubes on the soles of their shoes,
they enter singing the Third World Debt Blues.
Poison poppy economists overstuff a hot casino.
Pizza vixens buy into the Great Pacific Way;
dive beneath the foam dome of a cold cappuccino;
trip the plastic fantastic like the good old days.
Beelzebub fires up an humungous gigglestick,
and plonks himself down in front of the telly.
The sizzle of a couch potato turning on a spit
is raising hell from beyond the gravy.
Like taxi drivers don't brake for a backless maxi,
False Memory Syndrome don't fake how it feels.
The magazine Death Mask of Princess Di unpeels
from sleep-starved eyes. Caucasian rowdy
caucuses, who don't look or act Māori,
take crash courses in bar management for singles,
handclapping to the beat of razor-blade jingles.
The Minister without Portfolio wears a flyaway
toupee from Sir Robert's Hairshirt Factory.
He's swinging like a soap-on-a-rope champion,
autographs the bestseller, *Rivers of Phlegm*,
and promises airbag flotation to move the nation.
Joyboy and Ecowoman relive their glorious past,
polevaulting to the top of the Panty-Hose charts.
Here's to anonymous supermarket shelf stackers,
who have no marquee value, so can't find backers
for capitalist plots or the State Welfare Funeral.

Spell it out with words of one syllable—
black and blue means I don't love you.
Iron Guts reads container-loads of hate mail
in silence punctuated by gurgles of stomach gas,
while the stoned PM telemarkets electric pūhā
from the Beehive on wheels, a fast-track racing car,
to an uncritical admass modelling pimple rash,
and don't tell me you don't know who you are—
hurdling Thighmaster, Abdominiser, Diet-Upsetter;
smoking your computer under the nuclear umbrella;
the poor recycled as clueless with no agenda;
everyone a worthy cause in search of a soft touch.
The sungunned celeb holds a fashion victim pose.
In baroque burgeramas, rococo cola kids
engage in an orgasmic billion burger binge.
From shoe-lift to facelift, one triumphant turkey-trot—
rat grows human ear; sticky-tongue tiki; cerebral cortex rot;
dog's leg cocked against the family tree; blind spot
of interchangeable identities; privatised history.

Poet Aster: Primary Producer

Hot pot burns Poet Aster's tastebuds,
but scoured Poet cleans out the pot.
Cracking open the egg of language,
Poet eats a hearty breakfast;
the pet of Poet licks the saucer.
Everything Poet touches turns to poetry,
even paging through the clichés:
Poet falls on a sword of words.

Poet, submariner, hears ping echo pong.
Poet, with the coy manner of an ex-con,
operating without a current poetic licence,
is Poet with a pretty rum conceit.
Pow! Pow! Poet does a party piece.
Poet, postmodern pot-thumper unbound,
apostrophises the posthumous status for
pot-menders and post-hole borers of yore.

Poet walks along spines, tips over the sky,
reads clouds, tales of weatherboard,
texts of gnawed bones, grasses' rumours,
sonnets of tarns, sheets of water.
Poet's catalogue is a gridlock of lines,
trickling from the icy sweat of the brow.
Poet, poised at the brink, awaits closure;
proud parent: the pitter-patter of tiny words.

Forever Barbie

barbie bumps and grinds
barbie wolf-whistles ken

barbie works out

barbie's black roots
barbie's linguistic imperialism

barbie does her nails
barbie just does
barbie knows best
barbie powders her nose

barbie's buns of steel
barbie goes on a diet

barbie bops to a lite blend of tropical muzak
barbie has delta brainwaves

barbie marches to the beat of a different drum
barbie swims with the recycled plastic dolphins
barbie takes up with strange life-forms

barbie flashes peace signs
barbie brains herself on the glass ceiling

barbie begins to deconstruct power
barbie becomes a barbed-tongue extremist,
flogging the flaccid phallocrats of the patriarchy,
until they cry auntie!

barbie emails the dotcom people:
yo, dotcom, feed da world

barbie realises she is pre-determined, culturally,
and goes to do aid work in the third world

yo barbie
because barbie just does
yo barbie
because barbie just does

Anzac Day

As at a gubernatorial swearing-in, or a convention
of ex-Prime Ministers, or a double-dissolution of trophy wives,
or swan-songs sounding out for Gallipoli centenarians,
or a Nam Vets motorised wheelchair parade in Gun Club T-shirts,

we are enabled by Steadicam gimbals to gatecrash
the Scratch-Lotto Olympians' Golden Casket Mardi Gras,
and to trumpet with jumped-up DJs, Kieren Perkins is going,
Kieren Perkins is going, by the grace of John Laws, to Atlanta.

There are dressings for salads and field hospitals,
remotes giving the flick to ninety-nine nicknames of God,
lumpenproles barging through chainstores like cockroaches,
ruby caterpillars crawling down Parramatta Road in the dark.

Swimming pools are agog with foam, dancing cappuccino
corroborees to squeeze through rusty holes in buckets
under gale-warning palm fronds and froth up as chlorine rain,
while cane toads croak deep-throated, wide-mouthed blessings.

Ladyfinger bananas beckon subdivisions game to swing out
on Tarzan vines towards monsoon laundries of damp clouds
stained yellow, like ivory thrones, or old cricket whites,
as whirligigs of the hanged boogie on in phosphorescent fungus.

A branded Australian meat pie of a face comes up,
a skinned kangaroo in the front seat of a cut-price Mazda,
or a jelly platter of Bronco brawn on a Queenslander,
or a wig of water worn in a showerstall of crucified tin.

Coax mates to learn ya and lean into it, bending an elbow,
stuffing graveyard pineapples into jute sack shrouds
with the help of stump vision. Get transportation for life
on rafts lashed together from 44-gallon drums and THC hemp.

The Fremantle Doctor, hosing along corridors, blew them in.
Perth purls through its split-pearl bubblers, digging existence
in precious handfuls out of wind-tunnels sculpted by oceans.
The dreamtime of Brett Whiteley paints the Bungle Bungles.

O how the fuzzy-wuzzy angels touch the dead heart of Uluru,
with snakes of lightning that turn airports into billabongs,
and Melanesia into maps of cultural melanoma, woven out of
British Imperial standards and the cry of the currawong.

Rosaries of fish flap their bellies on prayer-wheels of trees,
frangipani slumber-parties float into sleeping sickness at low tide,
as the Nimbin glitterati tear strips off Royal Commissions
with syringes, detumescent trickles, and doctored urine samples.

Sir Robert Menzies stocked the fridge with treasures
from the Ming Dynasty; then Keating wound the clocks.
Now, lifesavers, chewing gum, comb gelled follicles into line;
and Australia, this Anzac Day, spreads until it stops.

Brisbane, 25 April 1996

Eternity: A Quick Sketch of Sydney

Cars bowl along in a tearing hurry to shave seconds off,
down streets the colour of opals, the colour of zoos,
streets the colour of your money, of your mirror sunnies,
streets crazy for curl, streets to bring you up short.

Stand by the side of the road,
getting sandblasted by the slipstreams,
and enough fumes to stun an aviary of galahs,
constructing personal songlines out of the mantras
of Sydney ascending.

Taxis take off like startled rosellas screeching
into a dream of oily gunk. Make tracks rote-learning
the sacred sites of Bondi, Edgecliff and Woolloomooloo.
Turnstiles ratchet as rail crowds file through,
hips foremost, like flamenco dancers.

Go walkabout, ambling or hotfoot,
into a Federation labyrinth, a scaly dragon's lair,
where sunlight undoes layers of lace and fades out snakeskin.
Roads boot-scoot around,
twisting like tourniquets, as the land runs to fat,
to skyscrapers, real big blokes, psychologically pulverising,
high-flying like topsoil into every corner of the sky.
Buildings are bludgers who won't budge,
not for a cup of snake-blood nor bushfire eucalyptus—
but are winched instead onto beds of nails,
anchored down in New South Wales.

Lizard town giving birth to magnetic clutches
of termite towers and ant-nest boil-overs.

Weird birds turn
above your paddocks, your padlocks, your Paddo dunnies.
Sydney, weeping sore, unbandaged boil,
you're a frigging finger up to century's end.
Seedney, with your essence of gonad,
what's that perfume you're not wearing?

Gutbuckets from hospitals burn in your incinerators;
your push-bike wheel rims are buckling under;
tennis rallies lob salvos of sweat at TV screens;
in nightclubs, missing persons rifle through coloured rain;
in bamboo cages, drug dealers mouth the word, Eternity.

New Year's Eve fireworks barge in at midnight,
spilling stars amongst jammed car-horn conga-line tailbacks,
and restaurant fish dead on sweating ice.
King's Cross blowtorches the dark with lighter fluid,
until an earth-cry at daybreak flashfloods the sky,
drowning the whole cosmological dreamtime in blue.

Sydney, 1999

Six Brisbane Snaps

Brisbane, bazaar of patchouli oils,
plus other strange stinks to spirit you back.
Ghost town, bedevilled by steak and kidney
aromas and faint chopping-block cries,
where cops gather like blowflies
in a muck sweat, putting the bogey to bed.

Sunbane, mandala of hot yellow flesh,
elasticated bandages worn with gold accessories,
humid skin floury with foundation powder,
wet with fragrant steam of evaporating alcohol.
Tree of ripe mangoes wrinkling to fulfilment,
where fruitbats hang like folded umbrellas.

Biscuit tin, weather vane pointed to sunny,
where glare strips paintwork, peeling gilt,
and old bugs dangle in dingy spiderwebs.
Beergut silhouettes on veiled verandahs:
at night the beds are burning,
sharing the secrets of the family silver.

Sinbin, on the move, flip-flopping,
skittering, scuttering, slip-slap-slopping,
click-clack. Small frogs climb walls;
butterflies flutter by waterfalls.
Scuffed lino teems with metaphors:
cockroach escapees search for the doors.

Fuzzchin, soft-stepping snake-handler,
shantytown of boomerang bridges over a river.
Train lines twine round in sap-sucking heat,

and crows grate through the long afternoon.
Scribbly streamers of bark spell warnings
of gold-hazed gum leaves, made to burn.

Brisbane, frame it round with fridge magnets,
glitter-glue its Xmas to your calendar.
The spray-on Santa snow has sunstroke,
the skin cancer clinic's boiled over and gone feral,
but endless waves are curling in, lyrically,
and their blue fathoms are freckled with light.

Southerly Buster

Psycho-active swimmer of lightning trees;
coral brain uprooted and flung fathoms deep;
Old Testament prophets in frenzied working bee:
a split-second light strobe to eye the storm.

Spat pip, pluck-pluck, hot steam-iron splutter,
luminous purple-velvet magic marker scribbles;
unearthing creeks, the thing flowers into a riddle,
kicking at the chook house with a kung-fu foot.

Draped silver mystery trains under frothy veils,
wedding showers with thunderclap assortments,
breezy sea-brides peeling off down cloud aisles
to meet a southerly buster rolling up the coast.

Rain so warm it oozes in a no-let-up guzzle,
a downpour backwards out from plugholes;
rain of the Pacific writing maritime testimonials,
filling volumes in libraries of soaked verandahs.

Overturned water glass, empty mould of wetness,
invisible skeins, fine-spun needles of nothing,
matting downy arms, trickling between eyelashes,
falling hard; rain whipped up until it tingles.

Republic of Fiji

Fringed by salt-water lace, the abandoned ship
British Empire drifts through Isles of Amnesia,
awaiting colonial mutual evaluation.
A shell roars inside the sea, calling to islands,
and islands surface like turtles in the rain:
rain white as mosquito net, white as grated coconut,
white as the helmets of ex-Governor-Generals.
Rain white like the walls of Suva city jail—
walls that hold bloody hibiscus, bruised mango,
and crims who blow smoke at a dead volcano.

Orchids nod to sermons of the wet season;
jungle is green ink bleeding into sludge.
Rain erases the movie of the great outdoors:
that soaked brouhaha of palm trees threshing
in a mare's nest of tradewind tales and trails,
as coconuts arc like basketballs for the hoop,
woven baskets' tropical plunder steaming.
Today's colour bar is scar joining scar to scar,
while anthill streets relay a taboo beat to
the black swish of Ratu Sir Lala Sukuna's sulu.

Suva's sweatshop sews all into one sharkskin,
when call of Shark-god pounding grog begins.
Muddy kava slurped up from coconut bilo
drives us further into earth at each small go.
It is land-divers free-falling to Pentecost;
it is skull-binders bound for Vanuatu;
it is rafts of pumice stones floating to Fiji;
it is a World War II submarine still undersea,

its encrusted fire coral and brain coral battery
lighting up the Pacific with republican dreams.

The red eye of the Cobra coil burns to nothing.
Degei spits a gob of gold into skies over Nadi,
and knocks heads of gods together, sucks out sap.
He shoulders a coconut sack, walks to market,
as if hauling an island along the sea's horizon.
Around reefs, black and white sea-snakes spiral.
The bula boys' shirts are prayer flags in rags;
Bure roofs are their top hats; Krishna's bus their chariot,
carrying them on firewheels whose spokes are knives,
along dirt roads where cane fields escalate into fire.

2000

FROM *FAST TALKER* (2006)

Water Views

Piled-up cumulus is gliding to nirvana,
and Dawn has on her bluest dress;
she's always seeking some brighter mandala
over silken banners of hot white sand.
The sea throws down her deepest green,
her surf is hissing like shaken tambourines.

Morning's child reaches to touch water;
sun-pointed deckchairs slope to the future;
in the bobby-dazzle the fizz boats prance.
People paste the seaboard in lashings of lotion,
limbs hug the earth with loving devotion;
through salt spray, with lyrical legs, shapes dance.

Sailors tack seawards on spanked-up yachts,
the sea throws spangles on bright-lit hulls;
the high tide surges with midday grace.
Trumpet flowers blare a yellow bossa nova,
sunbathers exist on the promised plateau,
wrinkling to fulfilment through afternoon's space.

The mottled skin of evening is drained of meaning.
Faces squint from verandahs to unseen horizons.
A wheelchair lies abandoned by the water's edge.
Shall we rise wise and free from this never-never,
and tumble-turn to torpedo to the far end forever,
under a perfect hemisphere of southern stars?

Summer Catamaran

Tāmaki Makaurau, mangrove-land,
your waters glug against wharf pilings,
shellback tidelines are your stretchmarks.
Salty city hissing between sea and sea,
I snatch glimpses of your panoramas,
air masses colliding like silky serpents,
thin grey membranes slithering with rain.
Subtropical, left to your own devices,
you set a cluster of arum lily cadenzas
coursing through the morning shimmer,
following the glassy curves of waves,
their luminous green fallings which lilt
to the shadowy beat of dragonish ships.
Heart rocking, the harbour cat takes flight.
Ecstatic, the mouth declares an interest:
to be anchored deep in the foaming drink.
Engines drum their fists to feed us
into the fathoms of the rippling current.
The boat is taking us into her confidence,
showing us the evidence, racing us away,
towards cumulus sailing high over the bay.

Titirangi Considered as Wearable Art

Fringe of heaven, half-clad in glad rags
of mist embroidered with drizzle,
your weatherboard, brick-veneered,
rubber-wheeled, possum-furred build-up
extends from roadways and bike trails,
from mown verges, and from ponga arcades
that, mud-stepped, down gullies parade
as if to salute shops along your main drag.

Bush suburb, spiralling, a fern provider,
you're decorated by wasps' paper nests,
and by pole-houses that want to flap out,
like wind-cradled box kites pulled taut,
while birds scatter-wheel to flutter
over canopies of trees rooted in legends
dug from the skull of the moa, and
hymned in the rasp of the cicada.

Silver sequins tremble on leaf-weave
of shawl draping your shadowy ranges,
and rolling to the lace of Tangaroa's sea.
Tangata whenua carved Tāne from kauri;
sawmill blades set the god free to change;
but he crumbled among moth grubs, breathing
out showers of sawdust in a kind of bleeding
to stain subdivisions that no longer believed.

Titirangi, your sunset blazes in amber resin,
your huia feathers gleam in museum gloom.
Ferns lose themselves; darkness finds coast;
a blurred kingfisher flees from a fencepost.

Eel-ladders descend to the world's womb:
stacked and storied trenches of Hine-nui-te-pō,
her kiln-like cave, from where shapes grow,
and the first frond of morning uncurls green.

Autumn Blast

From a high rostrum conducting tantrums
the wind polishes bluff and counter-bluff,
brings feathery rain to muffle dry leaves,
blows crumbs of cookies from cafe tables,
leans iron grillwork against pitted graves,
and barrels round rusted incinerator drums.

It rattles roofs like quick steeplejacks,
pummels wool beanies, gets under golf caps,
makes business shirts tucked in flap loose;
sly, it cat-licks corners of squinting eyes,
and flows a finger touch over ears across lips,
sibilant as stewed tea sucked between teeth.

To pinged road signs yellow as gorse,
wind sings, to slouching lanky schoolboys,
to earth mothers, too, whose children
running, circle them like gleeful moons,
to powerlines, airstrips, and the see-saw sea
carries its hoarse tune, to farm and to fleece.

At last the gale croons through the mānuka,
which twists and turns and seethes in its roots,
the storm gathering up skerricks of cloud
shadow, like merino yarn dyed deep indigo
and spun into a nightdress that, weighted
with rainfall, is put through the wringer.

Ode to Magnetic South

Place where culture signs its mark with thumbprints;
place of the moa cave egg sold for a hundred guineas;
blowsy, rooted place of meat going maggoty in a safe.
Zone of a late muster of Anzac stragglers;
zone of Kate Sheppard's white camellias;
zone of a galaxy of glow-worms galaxiids swarm beneath.
Keep of the blotted pages of damp explorers' journals;
lair of the feathered judge of the hanging valley,
swamp harrier riding the sky's fiddler music down;
lode of a spider's crawlspace where a fly's wing winks.

Ground of yarn, of unwrought aluminium, of sausage casings,
of crude petroleum, of urea, of inedible tallow, of casein,
of beer and wine, of kaolin and methanol, of tyres and shoes.
Ground of Packham's Triumph; ground of visitors' centres;
ground of ten Kates equalling two Apiranas, or one Ernest,
and all fluttering like butterflies into shop tills.
Ground of live horses, of sheep, of meat fresh
or chilled or frozen, of boneless beef, of veal,
of carcasses of mutton, of edible offal,
of prawn farms in power station cooling ponds.
Berth of dragnetted chainmesh and cordage
dripping a cherished mass of the unshelled;
berth of seawater curtaining in bubbles the grey mako.
Atlas of rivers up a bit, dirty, and running swift;
terrain of a fog softer than a cream sponge,
softer than a floury scone.

Tract where lichen grows over the brain of a rock,
where a hillside flukes its outcrop's claw,
where fence battens lean at all angles,
where tree boles buttress mountains,
where scrums of bees brace before nightfall.
Hemisphere where bright crust
rises into ocean light,
rises into volcanic dust,
into troposphere,
into stratosphere,
into atmosphere magnetic south.

Snow at 2 a.m.

Hazard leads the way, blossoming ahead,
to the moment grace tilts towards sublime
snow's slow dance on night-time's stage.

Three Japanese students run out in their
white underwear from the backpacker lodge,
brocades of ice sifting through their giggles.

Quantum sky-burial, abstract and bright
mystery practising the art of concealment,
snow's ghost ships, shrouded, sailing into dark.

Then an empty, green-lighted, silent street,
crystal interiors of freezers on surfaces of cars,
the clear sky alive with shooting stars.

The Scenic Route

The sales rep as off-road warrior
is zooming across the sheep's back,
where argonauts of the golden fleece
conjure broken ranges of a green utopia,
bonsai forests of coffee-mug trees,
ashen snowdrifts of province histories.
Anzac poppy harvests in skunkweed sacks,
held by skateboarders shooting the breeze,
travel the scenic route through old Karori;
newspapers thick as trees carry the story
to ngā rangatira slipping on cowpats.
Clinical foetuses model designerware;
rugby stars glue mobiles to cauliflower ears;
Adam Smith's invisible hand scratches DJ tracks.

The Bush Paddock

The sharp edges of tourist brochures cut to the quick, slashing away, down the
back of the bush paddock;
King Kūmara slithers from a sack of dark earth and begins to propagate his
progeny, down the back of the bush paddock;
most of Māoritanga is under water, and we live amongst its tallest peaks, down the
back of the bush paddock;
ladies bring a plate of butterpats, or do a terrific pavlova bake, or lather up a froth
of Rinso flakes, down the back of the bush paddock;
the greying of the nation sees grannies going for two dollars a kilo, down the back
of the bush paddock;
the hydrangeas are flowering in red, white and blue for the Royal Walkabout,
down the back of the bush paddock;
a department store is draped wall to wall, floor to floor, with black wool cardigans,
down the back of the bush paddock;
a railway station master raises his flag and blows his whistle for the Treaty of
Waitangi express, down the back of the bush paddock;
tribes of possums come up trumps, a pack of bludgers on the land, down the back
of the bush paddock;
a wandering prophet named Pākehā will eat the tongue and eyes of an enemy with
the heart of a cabbage tree, down the back of the bush paddock;
two drongoes are trying to build a replica of Mount Ruapehu out of playing cards,
down the back of the bush paddock;
Victorian outhouses get flogged off at outlandish prices, and sinister garden
gnomes lurk in the shrubbery, down the back of the bush paddock;
the parliamentarian with the head of a kākāriki strops his beak on a kōwhai tree,
down the back of the bush paddock;
a farm Cinderella and an old sundowner are dancing an Armistice jig to a
concertina, down the back of the bush paddock;
ups-a-daisy with the old lemon-squeezer, down the back of the bush paddock;
a horned thumbnail dipped in tar strikes a light to standing block, setting aflame
the beard of a bard, down the back of the bush paddock;

enough posts to prop up the scrum, the mine, the bridge, and build a pub for every man woman and child on the West Coast, are being milled, down the back of the bush paddock.

Old Railway Line to the Maniototo

The immense lilac storm just after dawn is a hive
of mating and hatching and growing wings,
fluttery white butterflies blown about
descending on trees and fields in shoals:
snow crystals, balancing the scales of morning
at highest point of the rail trail,
while a crop of cyclists
with twenty-one speeds to choose from,
plenty of elbow room,
bowls downhill like buxom apples let loose,
all crisp ecstatic yells and flaming cheeks,
towards Wedderburn's ex-goods shed,
a tin cave to whistle up a wind blast,
in a highland skirl of bladders
and bone beat on stretched skin drum,
as flurries of sheep clatter;
and goldenness of grass out of crusty mud,
that sunshine burns its way through to at last,
spreads from the remembering ribbon of gravel
and the bike spokes' windmilling thrum.

The Fencers

Ōamaru marooned in the South Island,
stalled in a holding pattern of summer insects,
inside your tameness there is music,
it is the harmony of the provincial,
where horn coils of prize rams carve into the mind.
Your cairns are the brushed-off crumbs of Arcadia,
to be remembered long afterwards by travellers
threading the white line of State Highway 1,
as the spindrift plume of afternoon drifts away.
Held together by the horizon, sawn out of stone,
not one of the Dominion's more disappointed corners
—Waimate, we're going past your turn-off—
Ōamaru, your architecture makes a stock exchange
of statuesque formalities in dumb, weathered grey.
Quarried memorial of fossilised whale eardrum,
your thunder sky is filled with seed granaries of ice.
Your earth is watermarked by puddles which mirror
dark branches to pierce the clouds with:
a swift-moving silent cinema turning sepia,
as evening climbs from its blind gravel roads,
rises over the sea and turns back to watch
the fencers, who plant axes and bury shovels,
before straining wire-strands until they balance
and frame a far-off view of mysterious space.

Drifting Cone

Under the slowly drifting cone of Taranaki,
when evening stretches out from the mountain,
the black tresses of its rivers wind me to you.
Always I feel the cold fire of your kiss,
that frozen fire that scalds my memory still,
the elixir of your lips where love fixed it,
so that I should taste, like tears in rain,
your distant indifference smouldering to ash.

I remember the scent of ferns you unknotted,
the crystal haze of mist whitely shimmering
on the sea-swell of your bare salty flank,
the mane of night on your shoulders of snow,
and the rare minerals of your eyes that flashed,
your distant indifference smouldering to ash.

Family Reunion

A child pushes out from the shallows,
submerged, then upwards showers
in silver slitherings as the pool gleams
its blue eye from suburban immensities.
Lawn-divers, we float and scheme
amongst worms to earth ourselves,
while steering our way between funerals,
where grief counsellors' profundities
about electrocardiograms or seismographs,
like promises of an unknown hereafter,
only lead further down familiar paths
wreathing around the hearts of flowers:
insignificance piled on insignificance,
before magnificence piled on magnificence.

So we, who had the chance to taste
the afternoon in a water-drop, found
time had become our prison turnkey.
We were held captive by our ordinariness,
while voids searched our fears and chased
us into the deep end of the mind.
We were children under the trees,
breathing in the bouquets of place,
peering into shadows interlaced,
until with slippery blueness we drowned,
and then, blurred with wild glee,
swam up towards the daylight glare,
forever racing the fleeing years,
forever caught by the rush of now.

Name of the Hurricane

Waves hit the breakwater, break like laughter,
lantern glass gets crazed, by cat-o'-nine-tails,
planks are yanked wise, from household nails,
to capsize caves of jails, in the twang of wire rails,
the rustle of tree flails, the whine of wind's veils,
as tossed grit of ashpits, bits of tobacco butts,
whirl above galvanised iron, prised,
and free tarpaulins torn, where branches borne
fight weightlessness, the way a crab grabs mud,
squelched on and dug deep, in that moment
when the ear hears mouthed faithlessness,
and the eye notes the bay, eerily calm of foment,
until again the rain, and bamboo cane brakes
thrashed to stashed mulch, as any croaks of regret
are stripped to mutter, with husks down gutters
of electrical fret, and in fronds unwoven
that shrivel cloven, stung by the sea
hung in the sky—those swaying beads
flung horizontally, to fray under
cloud mattresses of clapped-out thunder,
where tide's rocks bare sharp teeth to air,
and sea spray scribbles the wilder shore,
spelling names of the hurricane over.

.

A Pacific Islander Reflects in Cuba Street

The face of Che Guevara lives on the torso
of Mike Tyson as a rippling flag of black ink.
Havana is a cigar end glowing red at night.
Cuba has become the taste of rum mixed
with sour sweat, where America pokes
its fat pistol against the skull of Fidel
and spins the barrel—click, click, boom.
Rust defines the tinpot grog dens of kava,
and those casbahs of Noumean Napoléons.
Papuans bare hearts to flames of loggers;
rare turtle shells stacked like trash vanish;
the sea pours from a beggar's upthrust hand.
Suva's a flaking ceiling of candlenut soot;
Dawn's mouth is burnt peanut ash spat out.
Honolulu is a cemetery of suncream-white sand;
plantations grow totem poles for genetic labs.
Each aid apologist turns tourist anthropologist
making televised sagas of gold medal arts.
Skin-divers seek rapture from deep-blue skies;
a necklace of hot pennies brands you half-caste.
Cashed up, paid off, we flew the clouds like gods,
leaving rap sheets stiff with dishonoured cheques
beneath a dunny-can rainbow of shimmering flies.

Hotel Pacific

Firewalkers' flames flicker
in the gourds of tourist skulls;
leaf shadows make pillows a chart.
Garlands wear out their welcome;
mosquitoes whine like Cupid's bad dart.

Dengue fever travels by FedEx jet,
but cargo cult diplomats still flee
the Hotel Pacific slowly.
Lizards cough beneath the floors;
guitars twang from wire-screen doors.

Pink cloud skims the horizon,
beer froth tips on glassy lager.
Viewed from the hotel verandah,
the ocean does crash-dive manoeuvres;
blowflies crawl the grubby louvres.

Chewed cuds of banknotes are flung
where harems of ships' sirens once sung.
Private agents of secret powers
suspend dreams of freedom
for children who gather hibiscus flowers.

Shark-callers feed the fiery furnace
with a chopped-down forest of Jonahs,
and the helix of the tribe twists
between the crests of firewalkers,
until rain starts to fall with a hiss.

Hotel Pacific, washed up in a shopping mall,
trawls into the neon glare of it all.
On the beach a military band
is searching carefully for the lost chord,
as laughter of raindrops snorkels into sand.

Distance

Perth exists, swimming in casserole heat,
a metaphysical conundrum on event's horizon,
a kelp-swirl spiral of starburst breakers,
a sandstorm of feather, claw and beak.

Perth thirst is the pith of sun-sucked stones,
white stabs of light from a fish-gutting knife,
hawk's dry wing-flicks over hour-old roadkill,
a restaurant mandolin's monotonous tones.

Perth's the steam of instant food courts
with soups of noodles and pork fallopian tubes.
Perth's the gin slings of faintly angelic sorts,
as a jumbo jet lazily through azure moves.

Perth's the old digger, shadily respectable,
slurping down a sludge of toxic cocktails,
before belching up a firewall of chemicals
to tinge the Swan River's red sunset sails.

Perth's tunnels, subways and arcades swirl,
insect streams through prim suburbs purl.
Perth disperses the desert's endless mosaic
into a prayer-mat pattern baldly archaic.

Perth lives on as the ledge-end of the scene,
the specific, unnamed, underfoot dream,
the pearler, true-blue, easterly-westerly stew,
a floodlight bonanza, a far shore still new.

Perth of flaked cockroach and fibre-optic hairs,
of shelled things, peeled things, things not there,
hulled deseeded ennucleated things without
things in them, at rest under burnt sky's glare.

Golden Boomerang

Those propped up staring out to sea,
in sunglasses and Speedos,
gnarled claw clenched round a stubby,
the other round a tube of suncream,
hoping to croak their last like that,
to cark it staring out to sea;

human beings as accelerated forms of geology,
anthropological constant of identical packages—
within each hot halo
a head ripens, all smiles;

terracotta convicts, sandstone bandits,
focaccia ram-raiders on the tiles
with their spat-out bits of lung on pizza,
squid lobes gibbering under juice of lemons;

and the swimmer, salt-scaled,
going the grope and thump of waves,
sun-cured skin a tattoo parlour
of dark blue bamboo, of lotus blossom,
of guavas big as temple bell clappers;

then those who tip their caps
who show their calloused palms,
whose mocking musculature
is running soon to glut, to fat,
or already caught by the rip
is shooting through
to big breakers further out;

and the milkshake sippers moving aside
for him who carries his surplus adipose lightly
towards the buffed bathers at high tide,
and for her of the shuffle and shimmy,
of the blue bikini bottom
furred with sand;

and all those happy-face moppets
who kneel to squelch bladderwrack,
aquaculture a-flitter between paddling fingers,
plus them over there in their sharking brigades—
chest-puffed choirs of lifesavers and flag-wavers,
then those egged on by be-denimed pie-eaters
to drag driftwood poker-work inscriptions
about good and evil into midnight bonfires,
as camel-jockeys turned inner-city taxi drivers
drive the black-tar heart with rain on the brain;

then those favouring the bare-legged look,
in spare leotards or chewed togs
or other yanked-at skimpy clothing—
those crinkly crocodile men sunning on concrete,
body language that of a piece of perished elastic,
sunning prone as prawns on fork prongs,
prone as window-dressers' lashings
of plastic handbags and leather beanbags;

and the presence of red menace and yellow peril
in the eyes of the white power blokes,
their snakebite venom a bile of loopy brain proteins,
their voices hopped up to sing
with a dive-bombing mozzie whine—
seasoned hard nuts bobbing in surf's heatwave,
a sky screaming blue murder;

then sunset's oceanarium of windowpanes,
where TV's toothy munchkins and teen spunks
pixillate together on another dud sudser,
while reflected commuters hurrying by
on the ebb tide of the stranded day gasp and flap;

       all those who dodder in walking frames
       near sagging verandahs and dry tanks,
       who shuffle with spindly shanks,
       with gold chains that clink,
       while others, bisque, statuesque,
       fish on pedestals of rock;

and the cool poise of the ultra-slim
who quote beer-belly futures,
straining at swung kegs all best beer-garden days,
in a standing stupor to chug them down,
eyeing good sports holding heads high
(sweat-plastered hair flat, sprigs going tap-tap),
eyeing blithering nongs in thongs choking on bongs,
the front-row forward who has really let himself go;

       then the semi-retired vice-den racketeers
       adrift on personal floating boozatoriums
       as the gloss comes off the fibre-glass pineapple,
       beady-eyed in their whitewashed preserves,
       hoisting up the waistbands of their shorts,
       rust freckling their chromium trims;

those doing it tough down darlingest Darlinghurst Road—
saintly silvertails talking to themselves in Serbo-Croat,
adrift in the kerbside jetstreams,
suspended in a state of weightlessness,
and reflected faintly in polished counter fittings
of fashionistas and baristas;

all the counter-jumping streakers in sneakers,
streakers with heat rash,
and the satchel-mouthed or purse-lipped
bureaucrats giving chase,
someone else's rug-rats tangled underfoot;
the sweating suits jounced by rail;
and those decanted into oozing nightfever—
debutantes with lipstick like frostbite,
the bodgie retread with delinquent slouch,
aiming a bouffant missile-cone at stardom,
showboaters tugging Nautilus machines on out:

       every one of them sunnily a-tang,
       compost determinations in clays and ochres,
       beachcombers of the golden boomerang
       as warpainted by Chief Fire Alarm
       with rainbow vapours of oilstains
       to colonise radiant futures of precise temperatures,
       proposed limbos of sedated calm,
       an eternity of glittering sandgrains.

Dust

On breath of wind,
red dust's imprint.
The percolator brings
a taste of charcoal.

Scorching heat sings.
To walk stirs up
warm eddies of air
as clothes hang lank.

Hibiscuses wither,
smell of mangroves,
the mud-glazed river.
Stains on concrete—
rust, chocolate, blood.

Above trees, scraps—
thousands of bats.
Out of melon-scented
buttery dark,
barbecue smoke.

Night lightning,
smack of hailstones.
In the downpour,
hordes of cane toads
splash along roads.

Surge

Noon's blank stare is golden and blinding;
thighs thresh through creaming soda surf;
water's harmonies stream down fluent skin,
lyrical droplets under blue sky's top-spin.
Each wave shapes a loop of crystal ellipse:
slithering lures of oceanic eclipse.
Swimmers crawl currents of the sea,
tracing arcs of immense possibility.
Then a view of the wide moment frozen,
fast shadow stealing in under the ocean.
From deep silence where bubbles boom,
out of the surge, risen from the gloom,
in squiggles and foamy jigsaw puzzle,
thrill of a dorsal fin seeking dazzle.

Poem for the Sunburnt

Skin of tide-watchers,
skin of towel-flickers,
skin of surfers' flexing toes,
skin of curling hands in rows,
skin of feet scrunched in sand—

sunburnt

Skin needing salves and cool creams,
skin sleepy with daydreams,
skin smoothed with emulsions,
skin bitten, sweaty with compulsions—

sunburnt

Skin of nosey noses, skin of chucked chins,
skin of pink rashes, of twisted grins.
Skin of the tanned, skin of the bold,
skin bare-templed, saggy and old—

sunburnt

Skin wave-drenched,
skin salt-prickled, cold-blenched,
skin whose freckles ignite,
skin brushed with evening light—

sunburnt

Skin soft with imprints
from elastic of togs,
skin hard with scars
curving over and down,
skin pure as elements
deep in the ground,
skin that yearns,
skin that burns—

sunburnt

Brightness

Along the gloss of the coastal shelf
drifts the taste of the ocean breeze,
and a perfume that pours
from trumpets of flowers.
Up there the sky smudges pastel blue,
as the sun's fire flexes
to climb like the flame
of a matchhead held aloft.
All the dancers of the silver meniscus
are streaming and ribboning across
green, glazed transparencies.
Epic fathoms edge their speckled
fingertips into the shallows.
Inside the cloud of the oceanic self,
soaked seeds begin to grow.
A golden comb teases foam against sand,
and the beach is dazzled
to see a sudden clarity begin to burn
through the silken morning,
leaving the world netted in light
that is caught, that is held,
and then drawn tight.

Clicker

Lines on Peter Black's Moving Pictures *of 1986 and 1987*

Skimming the highway tarseal frontier blur,
travelling in the direction of time's arrow
into yesterday's immediate hinterland
—reflex action photographer's quick eyes
darting towards hints of the enshadowed
cultural debris of the past's residual creep—
the photos fizz with electricity of the moment:
each date-stamped pulse-rush-vibration stopped,
like a frozen cascade of flung fountain drops.

Their thousandth-of-a-second, look-see starkness
celebrates not just the lucky-shot cult of the car,
but the disembodied energy, the mad gallop itself:
the memory-sensation of a decade when the pace
began to pick up and isolation was overcome
by speed, the arrival of the satellite dish
heralding a global soul connectiveness,
as did corporate tokens of multinat franchises
and self-conscious broadcloth of business suits.

We are borne by a pilgrim swarm of incidentals
into memorial New Zealandness (not cute, ugly rather),
where flags hang limp on their standards,
zeal catches the nap and weave of small towns,
fluffy clumps of sheep tackle bungalow lawn,
and a cow's neck extrudes through slack fencing.
Slipping the black blotch of the rear-view mirror,
the leaden glare, the vaporous murk, the cryptic joke,
roadside attractions disappear off the windscreen.

Buildings' flaky prefabricated newness already history;
real gone the punk displacement of a nation in transit,
which moves as if zombified by voodoo economics:
the kids who squat like possums on fenceposts;
the soldier with mismatched footwear; stalked skinhead;
men and women with bags and suitcases walking;
mental furniture removalists; garage sale determinists;
and the dog raising its quizzical muzzle, its wet nose;
its eager light-filled eye meeting that of the camera.

On Ice

Strange attractor,
this predator,
as if the polar wind
was to plunge its tongue
down your throat and find
its way into your lungs
to lick all lobes
one by one,
turn them stone.

Home to pure science,
this palace.
Terns stitch its ceiling,
and skua wingbeats lash.
Berg giants
raise anchor for open sea,
amid wave splash,
chandeliers,
all the bling.

Illuminations
of crystal interiors,
mazy glitterings
of reined-in light,
here is the Antarctica
you were looking for,
the place
where nothing
escapes the white.

Reflection within the Frame

There he is buffeting,
punishing panes again and again,
with a damp shammy,
allowing defenestration
by impalpable luminescence
its maximum opportunity,
and also convincing impartial onlookers
of the earnestness of this window-cleaner,
which the lambent openness of his gaze
seems to confirm.
You look into him, through him,
see him, and do not see him
burnish a transparent corner of the world
at mid-morning,
the squeaky rainbow of suds flicked away
into a bucket,
as the sun shines and the day hurries on.

A Birthday Suit

Skin like turtle shell,
skin like sandblasted reindeer on glass,
skin like snub silver,
skin of tallow, of damask, of alabaster,
skin alive with a bronze patina.

Skin in Gabonese ebony, in ormolu, in ivory,
skin of leather, of lacquer, of veneer,
skin like camphorwood, like crushed eggshell,
skin as thick as the Maharajah of Indore's jodhpurs,
skin of gazelle-leaps and sunbursts,
skin in shantung, in shagreen, in rusted chrome.

Skin as a dustjacket, skin as a scourge,
skin as a scoop collecting the taste of the sea,
skin in rain, pitted and soft its grain,
skin like gardenia petals, skin like silk sheets,
skin with its mystery, earthy as a mineral,
skin with its history, stained like a criminal.

Ode to a Tooth

Grinning at eternity
from palisades of enamel,
cracked mini-altar on which
to the gods of energy and traction
so much food had been offered up,
you were selected for extraction.

Grinding ice pack
molar in the lower left quadrant,
where there's now a cave of pulp
soft as a sucked wine gum,
you were dragged by pliers
out of your place at the back.

Routed from the cotton mouth,
even anaesthetised, you resisted.
As the dentist levered the brittle
fragments they had to be spat,
leaving a burble of shaken-out,
bloody lacework spittle.

Polar, pale as dawn light,
I colour you gone for years,
though dreams of you still roam
my skull at night,
and every now and then my jaw
clicks like a gambler's dice.

Tulips

Flourishing at dawn,
rank upon rank,
they mass in cadenzas,
and glow like kisses,
embroidering mists
with blushes.
Their petals,
unfurling
from damp earth,
dazzle canals.
Flamboyant carousels,
cosmetics in drizzle,
let them tingle and flash;
let them float and sizzle.
Let them shiver and chime
beneath a dull sky;
day-heralds in turbans,
let them sing as we race by.

The Colour White

Fingertip reef,
cumulus ascending,
contoured smoothness of marble statues.

Ocean combers breaking in mist,
swizzles and spills of champagne foam,
beer suds forming moustaches on top lips,
a bride gowned in antique cream tripping
to iced wedding cake resplendent on table linen.

Swoon of midsummer's glare glowing,
fallen frangipani petal stars,
bleached bedsheets hung in the sun,
smiling jackets of porcelain teeth.

Juxtapositions of magnolia and jasmine,
dreamy harmony of blossom,
highest note of a melody in cascades of jazz.

Vanilla sundae, marshmallow, sugarloaf,
meringue beaten into soft peaks,
threads of coconut flesh grated in heaps
like trimmings from a ream,
the arena of paper where these words burn.

When the year turns,
breezes sing lemon and salt of the sea,
and airborne eiderdowns
of dandelion clocks puff along,
like a man whose hair is tufts of cotton wool
floating up into wisps,

sailing in raw cotton T-shirt, plain cotton pants,
catching the breeze like a seagull feather.

Gusts carry sleet that stings like quartz grit.
Snowflakes flurry their cold socialite kisses.
Morning blows out its cheeks and breathy vapour.

White is the abstract thing,
indistinct thing, luminosity.
Phosphorescent alpine ridges,
fires of constellations in the Milky Way,
crunches underfoot of lace frost,
back catalogues of packed snow,
winter's slippery citadel.

Midnight showrooms of whiteware,
brand spanking new, yet all alone.
Nurse uniform, photo-negative, pigment,
honesty, innocence, candles, incandescence,
soft lamp light, stark bone.

White
white
white
white
white.

The Book Reviewer

His tatty raincoat conceals a country,
rolled-up sleeves reveal many wristwatches,
he airily waves away rainbows of neckties
and pulls a smoke from a dark pocket.
But his book-side manner is a corrupt text,
for, though professing no fixed ideology,
he is a creature of isms and wasms,
sibilant with pure vexation, and even now
he is trimming his wick, getting the book in focus,
preparing the performance, his pile of cadences,
his cadences which lurk like police officers
preparing to mumble a caution of nouns,
or like chefs proposing a sticky syllable pudding
from the quicksilver promise of someone else's words.

News and Weather

Solemn chorusings of hair-on-end violence;
twisted hankies that scoop confessed moments;
soft-soap unction kneading careful silence,

while the run-to-ground smile, but look nervous.
Gaseous chatter formulating around them,
monsters of the deep are brought to the surface.

Birth pangs, growth spurts, hunger strikes, bills;
bursts of bullet points as balanced statements;
beautiful pilots zooming in for distant kills.

Then weather forecasting the motherlode:
flare-ups, cascades, dry spells, big blows,
and fiery comets falling by the bucketload.

In the Godzone

Zen managers from the Province of Bloat
gather wool off the backs of mountain goats.
Caesar's daughter in her tin chariot snaffles
the shiny kingpin of a million meat raffles.
His run carrying butchered cows' heads
stops its conveyor belts at a forest's cut edge.
A museum display of salad bowls courts
abominable snowmen of our ski resorts.
Anarchists climb the Beehive to reach
honeyed hexagons of Bumblebees for Peace—
                              in God's Own Country.

An opera diva indicates that her hair-do
is an art peak of mana to aspire to.
Thumbs of armchair pundits on mood swings
clamp the joybuzzers of Game Boy golf swings.
Scattershot pop-ups on universal internet
want to vend intervening eyes of poppets.
Boy racers hurtle; speech particles dangle;
celebrities huddle; reporters shoot angles:
all kinds of things are avid for rental—
                              in God's Own Country.

Beached whales of ex-PMs condemn
the roar of dollar bills plus the force of them.
South Island is taxed by rattles of phantom limbs;
North Island by nosebleeds of dehydrated crims.
Eyelashes shimmer on glossy globules of blood;
puckered foreheads think about bonds of love.
Think tanks pump rhetoric into dance clubs;

chainstores offer flea circuses for jitterbugs;
box-office poison gets doled out with ticket stubs—
                    in God's Own Country.

Daughters of the late colonial era dig up links;
paper tigers drown under lids that sink in red ink.
Digital dragons sail on oceans of ones and zeroes;
baa-baas gambol through slo-mo pastorals.
Televised broadcasts using night-vision goggles
reveal an entire nation playing possum;
scenic calendars burst into gene-modified blossom—
                    in God's Own Country.

Body Clock

Fireworks chandelier, glitter of a disco sphere,
sparks-encrusted rind of earth peeled clear,
mystery envelope holding another New Year—
and the winner is nineteen eighty-four.

Steamrolled by heat, tar bubbles burst;
mineral waters bless the chrysalis kiss of frost;
shadows of wings dapple pavements, gum-embossed,
and nineteen eighty-four's numerals of polished brass.

Fathers tense, taut like champions caught in a hug.
Mothers advance in regiments and troop unknown,
their tear ducts stuck open but still all smiles.
Children take off and belly-flop in tattoos
of splashed indigo laced with silver surf,
scar tissue spelling nineteen eighty-four.

A sky god rips featherbedding until snow falls
on bulwarks of ocean and alpine palisades.
Purse-lipped, forever winding, wind glissades
and writes on itself the quivering score
of the nihilism known as nineteen eighty-four.

Nineteen eighty-four, the hotline phone number
crank call Reagan makes to Andropov the year
Indira Gandhi dies and Lange has his finest hour;
micro-circuits gong out doomsday in Hollywood;
bolts of red carpet weave sticky with body fluids;
the press corps syringes through the eye of a needle
to squirt the gravity of each heartbeat in marble.

Poor representation; turn-offs not taken;
doublethink; disconnected lip-synchronisation;
memory's sorry slipstream; Orwellian racketeers
hoisting the date off its rusted bracket poignant
as an empty mini-bar, cracked display cabinet,
ruptured fluffy dice, lost stash, one-way glass,
boarded-up dump, or garden wire-netted and long
beneath grass; inhale exhale nineteen eighty-four.

Nineteen eighty-four, bigger than *Ben-Hur*,
a time-lapse photo-shoot fogged in light,
ragged skull-and-crossbones on a distant shore,
a flame-burst of energy swallowed by the sun.

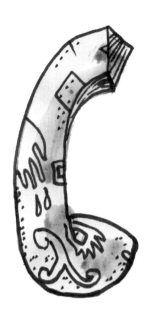

FROM *TIME OF THE ICEBERGS* (2010)

Birds

Flock
at sunset,
message flung skywards,
shreds
into the dark
alphabet.

On Beauty

after Charles Baudelaire

You, scarred wahine, lift pounamu profile,
wearing a cap of plumed indignation:

leaf tannins of creeks rush across your tongue;
smoke from burn-offs wreathes your sensual

undulation, pelvic girdle of volcanoes,
forest mists—your rivers that midges sing.

By katipō's kiss, shimmering black and silver,
we're held, but in an embrace distant and hard:

your whenua yearns to tides and moon's glow.
Matrixed with ferns, your surf's tow rips under,

as Anzac horses might, on war monuments, prance.
Gales through mountain rifts moan your praises.

Between deep fiords: landslips of slow footsteps.
Lakes dark eyes, you triumph in your screen test.

At Macraes Flat

See the round hill's lone tree planted for war dead,
who soldier on year after year, though gone;
yesterday's clammy fog blown free, tufts anchored
tentative, like lambswool snagged by dry thistle,
or suds from wash-tub rest-cures for work clothes.

Caught off-balance, a bumblebee falls to dart
from the car whisking through butter-and-egg-yolk light
making golden rabbit pie crust, thyme's hare sauce;
windscreened rush past tussock pulse, lake bristle,
bleached peaks, stacked stone house roofless in sunshine.

Rubbled sheep exercise their right to be a flock.
Curved like clouds, hiding skinks, rocks emerge,
ribbed as if scarred by frost snap, hail scratch, wind grip.
Their sky-staring angles patched with flaking lichen,
silhouetted heads of petrified gods, they stud slopes;

and rise from craters dug deep, daffodils dust-caked,
pig pelts hung to cure on a farm fence by the hundred;
while haulers jolt schist, drag ore searched for by blade-tip;
till, the whole day shredded down to sea level and dark,
the car follows the road along a cracked-open spark.

Warming

Up here,
seagulls float like kites on thermals.
Down there,
a car canters like a racehorse
through pasture, towards Aramoana.
The giant wharf cranes of Port Chalmers
stand like steel giraffes in a story book,
and time is reluctant to turn the page.

A fishing boat's wake is
carving a V
in the freckled salty skin of the sea,
furrowing its calm green translucence,
until the sun squeezes juice from quarter
of a lemon onto the veiling, foam-white,
dissolved wings of a billion butterflies.
Pick up that foam, pick it up and drape it
across the dry riverbeds of the skies.

The Harbour

Rainbow's edge soaks up time,
December opens its album,
we welcome days with flowers,
form clouds to thread high tides,
silver touches our fingertips,
freshest almonds press their oils,
and cordite is a valve for fire.
Eyes sewn tight with teardrops,
violet penumbras under lashes,
the point of her tongue a bustle
of fizzy atoms, blood oranges,
rare earths, trace minerals,
pepper, clove, cinnamon, her
skin smelling of petrol and tin,
we hear the radio play house,
house keeps it under its hat.
How to harbour a harbour's Sunday,
its woolly Zeppelin self aloft?
Bees, a team in striped sports kit
unbundle their goal-questing as
an embrace of wings around apple
blossom crowding the panes that open
on harbour's steely water, darkened
to the shade of the windscreen of the
red car towing a speedway wreck
by trailer along Portobello Road.
Brewer's mash, coal smoke, sugar drift,
a late burst of cadmium lemon light
when afternoon greases up to evening,
and the harbour's turquoise cathedral
shimmers, as if covered with fish scales,

or frocked in satin of Virgin Mary blue,
before turning amethyst as evening's sky,
then ebbing, weed-woven, stinky, stapled
in by rusted ironmongery and bitumen,
crumbled clods risen to an old church
with sharp steep pitch, above which
muscular hills flex before falling away
to crumpling surf, white sheets on a bed,
ocean breathing out brushings of wild silk.

Graveyard School

Harpoon spires, coal smoke, iron rustbucket,
daylight's bright fine gold, cranny of the South.
Judgement's dungeon cell, lost hospital maze,
tiny ark with cabinets of curiosities padlocked.
The lone piper able to bring the young running
the nexus of street veins to the octagonal heart.
Then submarine arcades, fleets of wooden shops,
sell-out sermons on oyster saloons ready to open.

But between pipe skirls and wool skeins stands a
boil-in-the-bag city, whose teaspoon-tinkle stanzas
announce fine china cups are running over absently,
populace gone in search of oats and possum stew.
Who'll buy clay chamberpots, a weighing machine?
If buildings are porridge-coloured, eminent stone,
go down into the catacombs: there the dead snore.
The gannet colony's a rest home, sounding out oracles.

Repeat the series of thirty-nine steps after Cargill,
from his named summit, street, monument, corner,
and watch last Century wash up in cinema lacework.
Ironmonger's nails swapped for a sack of earth that's
sewn into a uniform riding through Canongate.
Under a shirt of frosty stars, the kilted hills.
An eight-sided poem spiders the crystal screen:
hail to the ears, the whole town gets up and cheers.

Tāwhirimātea, God of Winds, Visits the Province of O

On this blowy evening in high summer,
all the tassels of toetoe are dipped in aura,
and tarry roads are pulling Dunedin taut,
like stout ship's ropes,
as if the whole brick-and-stone shebang
was about to launch oceanwards
in search of some further shore,
with the expectant sky
holding the risen moon's thin scythe,
for harvesting pumpkins,
watercress, clumps of borage,
wild blue flowers flickering.

Clouds, white as the paper bags
wearing the initial of McDonald's
blowing in the wind down George Street,
turn gold in dying rays,
like tattered battleflags of brigades,
whose remnants lodge in cemeteries
the length and breadth of the Province of O,
in a region given over to remembrance,
through war memorials and parkland statues,
of a lingering imperial past.

And, as a nor'wester swirls through the asphalt
jungle of North East Valley
between houses ploughing down the green swell
and up the other side like flotillas of boats,
lifting on its buoyancy, on its updraught,
supermarket carrier bags full of wind,
full of the breath of Tāwhirimātea, god of hot air,

the gliders have descended at Ōmarama,
and open-tops of sports cars have closed at Ōamaru,
for Tāwhirimātea has begun to gallop along the coast
like Four Horsemen of the Apocalypse,
like the Hounds of Heaven, like the Grim Reaper,
and with pentecostal force divine on whirlwind tour,
become the twister travelling through Kurow
that picks up a herd of kunekune pigs
to transport them shuddering down the road,
while cats cartwheel to use up all their lives,
and trees dance fandangos branch to branch.

Tāwhirimātea the dust devil flings horseshoes,
scraps of rust, and howls outside doors of pubs,
and hurries off in all directions to arrive everywhere at once,
and with one last gesture dumps, like barrels of bowling club
champion rosettes, a ruddy sunset glow
over the ranges of the Province of O,
till, next thing, night turns off the light,
so the glow is stuffed and Tāwhirimātea runs out of puff,
and no windmills turn, and no sails arc,
and the Province of O's becalmed, floating in the dark.

Dada Dunedin

For	I will consider Dunedin, for you are a brackish backwater inhabited by South Sea gods.
For	tipped out of a colonial toy-box, your stone buildings mingle with the bones of the land.
For	oystercatchers by night, above Knox Church, cluck and chuckle, flying seawards.
For	you have villas, with diamonded mullions blazing, and glossy cast-iron lacework whose doily fringes hang above verandahs.
For	you have villas decaying and tomb-like, mantelpieces crammed with empty bottles and medication.
For	Robbie Burns in bronze plucks a quill from a passing gull, and writes on air words in praise of Octagon hip-hop.
For	at your centre you have a shiny Gaggia espresso machine.
For	within your castle keep are the witch hats and wizard cones of pinnacles and turrets, cloak draperies, and a vault possessing the Harry Potteresque desk of the Ettrick Shepherd James Hogg.
For	your bees nuzzle summer's clouds, and your skateboarders scrape out pavement's song, and shadows drawn from trees run across your parks in the late afternoon.
For	Jetty Street on Sunday is loud with the eerily magnified musical whispers of industrial rust, and guitar fuzz buzzing like sourly ground-up sawdust.
For	Anzac poppies bloom in Picardy Street, and orange cordials are poured on Alhambra's sports fields.
For	every other corner on Princes Street echoes to bagpipe skirls, horse hooves clatter, and the phantom flow of golden syrup ragtime piano solos.
For	Rattray Street remembers the boogie-woogie, the elective jazz mutes, the wah-wah pedallers and the doesy-does beneath zigzag steps.

For   King Edward Street is greasy with the taste of Southern
        Fried Gothic, and loud with rugby choruses from beer-
        babblers at the Brook.
For   your seagulls glide up and down George Street looking to
        greet all they happen to meet.
For   your mollusc-like dwellings are concealed by tough thorny
        hedges.
For   you have your pipe dreams of a harbour bridge
        and railway tracks elevated above a statue of Queen Victoria surfing.
For   you still possess the ruined grandeur of some cavernous
        Edwardian gin palace populated by elderly alcoholics.
For   you are a synonym for depopulation, petrified as limestone,
        with your buried tunnels leading to bricked-up bomb
        shelters and closed gold smelters.
For   you are a clue to all of New Zealand, a primal bog of
        settlement which has evolved to spawn many of the nation's
        symbols of self-identification.
For   who knew what could grow inside your cocoon of will and
        idea.
For   there are rumours of beetles munching their way through
        your museum, over the notched spears and sandstone
        sinkers, the basalt adzes and bones of birds.
For   you are a jester in cap and bells holding up an inflated
        gallbladder on a stick, which vibrates in the wind like
        an aerial tuned to otherworldly hymns.
For   in the New Year you are a ghost ship of a town maintained
        by a tatterdemalion skeleton crew in op-shop regalia.
For   the sight of you spread out in the skylarking sun reveals
        postal districts packed with concealed email users.
For   you stretch up, Dunedin, take a breath, and sunk in
        dreamtime vacancy seek to break the trance of a hundred
        years, aware in your cobwebbed obstinacy that you're
        making an exhibition of yourself again.

Heraldry

Hand upraised beneath a cloak of mist,
the colonial goose is cooked and eaten;
triple-chinned wonders soak in thermal springs,
and seals bask on Zealandia's sundeck.

Loneliest place on loneliest planet,
where bees quilting sew pastures silver,
dairy queen udders burst snowy from alps,
and pine cones cast-off await collection.

Dip your toe in Marlborough wine lakes;
dodge falls of rock climbers out of mountains;
read small grain of a given piece of timber;
and wad cardboard into rugby ball shapes.

Blood sport jokers jockey for lunch money;
tractor blockades smoke the Beehive out;
pre-mixed under-agers gatecrash winebars;
and blat of grrrl racers burls down boulevards.

Fox Glacier launches a hot fridge brand;
fine wool clouds gather fattened lambs;
paddock barbed wire's bent round in a crown;
and urgent hayseeds gee up Race Cup steeds.

A name that ripples in red, white, blue;
a slippery pill popped from a seething scrum,
half freezer pack, half frozen shoulder;
and ref's whistle to raffle off a brassy win.

Weet-Bix bards at breakfast address their mums;
hip-hop stutters through blizzards of abuse;
snowboarding bohunks neck ekkies with glee;
and all eyes on screens fix, as if held by glue.

The Five-Cent Coin

A puddle of silver makes a tumbled host of tuatara,
spun on wooden counters, dropped five-cent coin.

Whence the hikipene, tickapenny, for soap, candles,
matches, for the paper, the milk, dropped five-cent coin?

When the whole world was the size of a gobstopper
summoned with a rap on a glass top, dropped five-cent coin.

Once it carried decimal weight and heft, handed down
from sovereigns and crowns, dropped five-cent coin.

Bob, copper, ding, electrum, shiner, tanner, zack:
passed on, pocket to pocket, dropped five-cent coin.

Legal tender, put money where your mouth is, accounts
due burn holes in pay packets, dropped five-cent coin.

It filled a gap, that shiny dot, pitched or tossed acrobat,
stuck to the pavement by chuddy, dropped five-cent coin.

Empty husk, a tiddlywink flicked to the end of the line,
the breeze light on sun-crinkled water, dropped five-cent coin.

Escaping to roll, wobble, travel into corners, spiral
once or twice, fall face down, dropped five-cent coin.

And still you see it here and there, in dust, or else gathered
and crammed into a jar for buttons, dropped five-cent coin.

Ode to the Beer Crate

Beercrate, part of landscape,
part of folklore memory,
staple of nostalgia.
Spartan, pragmatic, transient, expendable;
low-cost, mass-produced, abundantly social.
Assemblage knocked together
out of a few short pine slats with nails,
sometimes with a logo stencilled;
used by breweries as a container for holding glass bottles,
simple, almost elemental, totemic box, airy crate.
Stacked at the back of a pub in storage;
resembling street junk, mute but everpresent.
Unlabelled, stacked wooden pyramid,
fragile, yet enduring.
Block-like grid of horizontals and verticals,
bearing resemblance to state houses of the 1940s,
which is fitting because they celebrate the egalitarian ethos.

Put to the purpose for which they were made,
heavy clinking crates that symbolise plenty,
a twenty-first initiation, a necessary
part of hāngī or wedding or barbecue.
Full of grog, boozebarn accessory, macho,
but not as macho as an aluminium beer keg,
and ecologically more sound
than plastic webbing and plastic wrap.

An empty receptacle, the second-hand beer crate drifts,
becoming a platform for a speaker to stand on and address a crowd,
an extra seat at a party,
a shelf supporting a vase of flowers;

then forlorn, ending up as scrap,
splintered to firewood,
fed to flames.

Kōauau

Oracles of mist reach
to sea-foam volumes
a feather touch
at the river's mouth,
breakers the only pressure
solitude feels
as evening's fronds
mark golden glare
on the brows of ranges,
moon's risen skull
grinning at a West Coast
so brooding and so dark
it might be made of coal.

Christchurch Gothic

Summer's Avon spelt the names of atua in green,
and through trees sun-shafts dug at dappled lawns,
as if to unearth a circuit board of wormholes,
the universe beneath the labyrinth,
the silent presence of mountain shingle
across the curve of the island's waist.

Teen racers hummed like bees in a hive,
and late autumn was the harlequin
hurrying past them down Bealey Ave,
towards the rusted, busted, midnight hour,
its sword-and-sorcery pageant of flashing sabres,
its chorus lines of black on moonlit runnelled iron.

They drained the swamp for bodies,
and found a city in a smog overcoat the colour
of mid-winter: a swallowed-up netherland.
Around it, paddock windbreaks rose in ranks,
long shadows falling like guillotines,
as night exhaled its nausea.

Frosted spring melted into this deep carpet,
and from Port Hills rolled the squared-away harvest,
whose matted roots expressed pedigrees of settlement,
a holding pattern of heartbeats, brainwaves, fingerprints
down blind alleys. The city breathed in—
a hot air balloon sailed above its festoons of bitumen.

Cricketers

In primary school I buckled pads on
to learn cricket's formal grammar,
how it built hours of prose, moments of poetry,
from architecture of six sticks, two small planks,
and the crack and smack of shot from pitch.

In the classic stroke, bat collides with ball,
which is hurled to hang in the outfield;
airborne it looms, avoiding hands of welcome.
The ball touches down alone, then is flung
in vexation back to its keeper at the wicket.

Dug in at the crease, I flicked at spinners,
but didn't often thump the earnest half-volleys
other boys served up. We were like chess pieces:
in white, on a green board teachers controlled.
Summer found us in long grass looking for the ball.

Forward to the Eighties, watching New Zealand's
eleven—legendary as Ian Botham's gut,
or broadswordsmen, or poets with Curnow's
wild iron—whacking Oz then England in Tests,
to make sinewy syntax articulate.

There was Hadlee, a scorching nor'wester
sailing from a clear sky, gusting at batsmen;
from his arms' bent longbow a red arrow
launched at the stumps, fielders arrayed like posts
of a pā palisade, ready with haka leaps.

Hadlee on stride, a catapult on one leg,
back leg a rudder, lobbed the ball so it bobbed
off-kilter, but sprang beneath the bat to shave
off bails, before batsman, slanted at the slats,
had grasped that the wicket had been taken.

And batsman Martin Crowe, who could help
the ball, once or twice, soar like the Remarkables;
or swat it away to the height of a hill;
or clobber the sphere square-cut for four,
shake his waka paddle, then just lean, weight on bat.

Glenn Turner sometimes swung a haymaker;
other times, all day, he built a stone wall,
but snagged the ball to steal a run or two.
He could lock up batting with strategic play;
with sure motion make the game drift his way.

Summer Hail

Summer is searching for shady verandahs,
fingertips moving over shrubs and crockery.
Each window fine-tunes a crystal angle,
venetians running cool stripes over greenery,
as time is knocked into the hat held out
by clowning child or grown clown's memory.

The dog is ropeable, he barks and barks,
at bulging garden hose, mad as the cut snake
that mimics a traffic-directing cop in motion,
or thrash of someone stood on the garden rake;
while our hands grab at handles, pluck weeds,
wring out togs, and wave for old time's sake.

Those black-and-white photos with yellow tint,
you have to dig down to where they're buried:
they show us kids going on an expedition;
playing backyard cricket looking worried;
or laughing squint-eyed against the sun's glint;
always holding out whatever find we carried.

A kitchen sieve clangs as if about to sift
heaped flour for sponge cakes of nostalgia.
Light heel-tap of spoon, roar of the mixer;
and the iron roof, rattling kettledrums
above rooms which darken when hail comes—
the rooms where shades of summer drift.

Winter, She Said

The tumble-drum drier churns
clothes you left when you left.
Tree frogs into dark waters leap;
skinks through bouldered crevices slide;
a dulcimer is strummed in the casbah.
Puff-cheeked clouds chase sunset's shadows
across quilted fields of Canterbury.
Wasps have built a paper nest.
Gloom surrounds the fading house,
and its chamber music of doleful door hinges.
Chopping wood in winter as wasps hum—
from summer's zenith it's a long way down.
Kindling unlatches
at the catch of flame—
stacked wood roars like an angry man.
Sawn-up coffins of nameless insects
melt to a red glow.'
Night switches on darkness
room by room;
recess rises from recess;
windowpanes glisten.
An anorexic moon
slips from a smother
of ferns, a cradle of branches,
and glides with a glimmer
towards a pincushion of stars,
leaving nothing but the touch of moths and frost.

Kate Winslet Promotes a Credit Card

She's contorted over script or contract.
She mimes reading with hunched back.
She's somewhere inside *The New Yorker*.
She poses beneath the legend: *My life, my card.*
She sucks, like a straw or claw, at her finger.
She exposes, like that of a great ape, a foot's sole,
wrinkled as a map of the moon.
She has a big toe that seems so much older
than the rest of her, as if she has just
arisen from a bath, and that big toe
was under longest.
She has that toe as the punctum,
so that we must contemplate smoothness
wrinkled in a bath: that wrinkled, sensitive
point of balance exposed; just out of its shoe
and already cooling the blood.
In a photograph the colour of greyish tin,
she feels through the sole's drumskin
each reverberant step of her life.
She's architecture; she's an archive;
she's a firebird; she's a poet's metre,
putting her best foot forward.

Steve Irwin Way

The Glass House Mountains float on the horizon.
Their strange shapes fill the morning.
They are rum casks rolled down from Bundaberg,
or old pagoda bells unearthed
from a ballasted world of giants.
Steve Irwin Way switches like a croc's tail,
and the shapes vanish as Noosa traffic roars.
Daylight is on slow burn, all grease vapour
and hot air, a sugar fix hitting home.
Reptile eyes surface from cappuccino swamps,
the hills wait to speak with fire's tongue.
Gums sift light and ooze hospital balms,
my sandals feel as slippery as mango skins.
Ironic caws of rooftop crows
sound out noon's scheme of things,
waves of stink ripple through the nose.
Leaves are gnawed into brocade by insects,
bark coffins sewn for their congregations.
High rollers run the sun's lucent comb
over surf shrivelling to freckled foam.
Surfers rise to cumulus peaks and pours
above ghostly jellyfish men-o'-war,
as if to join the white-bellied eagle's soar,
then tumble like pigeons towards an ecstasy,
a rush of bubbles, the laughing Buddha of the sea.

Belief in the Pacific

Yes, night's nowhere, that's where I sleep;
till the sun wakes, stretches, begins to burn,
and greets me when my eyelids, dazzled, leap.

Sunday's hymns laze on ocean's horizon.

Cloud feathers sand white, as green seethes
across taro leaves, across palm fronds' weave;
and coconut trees vault to the blue sky
clang of church bells.

                      A man bows to consult
his Bible; thumbs verse like a hitchhiker,
smooth brow filled with lagoon's light,
though engine drone drowns surf's sigh.

From sleep's hurricane my mind heaves
its woven mats; and I'm this wind-drifter
with fraying map, dreaming of a comeback.

Soundings

Caught in the ear of the wind,
silence stretches for an instant,
then to summer's racket succumbs:
children shrilling out a need;
a doorbell by hawkers thumbed;
pavements alive with clicking heels;
the cool white noise of news, urgent
to natter and bleed through walls.

Growl of bus, beep of car horn,
construction sites to eavesdrop on;
generations making dissent and din—
whine, groan, roar, moan, hum.
Sounds spelling it out as song:
shivery nuances, rising pitches,
acoustic ripples, transmission glitches,
snap of teeth and bubblegum pop.

The uphill grunt, the glottal stop,
the hit tune warbled from the shower,
while furtherest stars since their birth
have been singing like a lawnmower
on a fine Saturday afternoon,
heard from so far away from earth
it's almost not heard, no more than
absent hiss on a sonic detector.

Yet we cheer them to their very echo:
sing you singers—the time of singing
is not over yet, so sing, echo on echo.
Sounds of many call over the bay;

carry me back, they sing to us;
and in the end all are chosen;
our songs lifted from below,
torn from earth to float away.

Oh that voice of God technique,
those chords of glory, that grandiose talk,
those notes raised by an orator leaping:
Holy musicola, and do-rag promises,
old hee-haw of the donkey caravan;
or snicker-snacker-snick of barber scissors;
Nazi bellow at the Nuremberg Rally—
a cut-off, chicken-plucking horrid squawk.

For the dolphin language, they say,
has twelve thousand semi-tones;
and there's a magic drone that blesses
those who feel it—*have you heard, have you heard?*
I have heard monkish choirs, skeletons tap-dancing,
seventy-six trombones, a hurdy-gurdy that swirled,
blood's steady drumbeat, polychromatic cellphones:
all sounds speaking with the mouth of the world.

Spent Tube

A cigarette after a long absence is like
revisiting haunts of my lost youth,
where I made a hollow claim or two in my time,
as the whole world danced to the same smoky tune
before we all swore off that infernal bridegroom,
that fictive fig-leaf curling up into the cut-
and-dried statement of ciggy threads set alight
and blazing at once like Balzac on caffeine,
us party-goers of manic erudition,
juggling wee small hours the other side of midnight,
where bees are smoked from bonnets
at the behest of rollies dancing in the hands of the voluble,
toccatas of talkativeness until night becomes day,
with gesticulated odes to Drum or Winnie Reds
beneath some tobacco god's revered smoked head,
tribute of such fiery tabernacles of tobacco
as to be a rakehell's cat-scratch fever sated,
yet still in love with its poisonous fumes,
its wavering mirages stitched from skeins
of wraiths wreathed into bleakly elegant pose,
its ash that deft fingers conjure dreams from,
in medicine man or peace pipe ceremonies,
glow of satisfaction below the level of language,
at smoko,
by the side of the road,
by a doorway, by a swill-bucket,
with a man who jokes,
trapped in rings of chain-smoke,
expelling voluminous puffs
much as if he's smoking himself,
tarry vapour sucked down off-kilter,

to calm jumpy nerves,
until it falls like a dud from nerveless fingers,
or from the lips of dying warriors,
the last heroic puff in a newsreel,
spent tube but still dancing spot of light,
because the cigarette I was smoking then
has not yet been stubbed out.

Beer Cans

There by cliff-top carpark we raise our beer cans'
                                    warm foamy ziggurat
to the slowly buckling green Pacific carpet,
                                    which sparkles its saltpans,
while birds flutter across the blue-eyed day
                                    like eyelash mascara,
and sunlight bounces on afternoon's trampoline,
                                    so joyously at play,
as marbled waves shoulder a rider in gleam
                                    of black wetsuit to shore.

Poked fingers point balance over a parabola,
                                    fathoming ocean curves,
before that crouched and slewed surfer, alive with nerves
                                    atop booming breaker,
on crest of lustrous liquids steps, to cartwheel,
                                    a da Vinci man stretched,
down through sudsy washing machine vortex,
                                    like a boat's ploughing keel,
then from crumpled page of the story-book sea climbs
                                    to paddle out once more.

Jailbird at Mōmona Airport

He kārearea ahau …

I come from the bay of hawks.
Propellers roar my tragedy.
I roar my own ecstasy.
I'm exiled where I walk.
I drool. I hang on my own talk.
I'm between jails coiled in a shroud.
Enter shackled at wrist and ankle.
My feet are bare. I rankle.
I'm off to where I'm sent.
But my stare is proud.
The howl of the mongrel.
The fool's toothless scowl.
My tinny shack paid back.
Tinfoil, flame and the glass bowl.
I drank. I trespassed. Now I rage.
I don't utter sounds of doubt.
My rhetoric is renegade.
I return to thoughts of dak.
I chew my cheek. I'm made.
My toes claw the floor.
I am silent as a waiting gun.
I stare at the sun.

Taranaki Bitter

Bitter rain barnstorms green's mean ark,
bringing a hairy eyeball to play on
the velocity of culture vultures, who talk
in offal accents of their new dreamland,
where it's the zeal of gods rolling their own
that is slapped down amidst hilliness,
ocean horizon's long grab at nothing.

Shearers wrestle sodden sheep off ute trays.
Lizards of steam climb the kitchen ceiling.
Lather's not strained as each glass is drained.
Choruses of bubbly streams traverse gullies
to echo the roar of a river's welcome,
while solitude of rain gangs up on all
gathered at Queen Tuatara's funeral.

Barnes Dance, Queen Street, Auckland

Crossing at the crossing on Cross Now,
where crossroads criss-cross, you cross
over crossing still, but lost to view
in crowds crossing now; crowd joins to
crowd in collective crossing, weaving
madly addled webs of rhythmic steps;
crossing and re-crossing rapidly reversed;
finding a personal way of moving, we
heel and toe it as it might be; trek to trot,
each foot as bulbs and root lifted up;
suits are jumping out of lifts to cross;
tripping, stamping, limping, we cross
back with the flow; lean and slide we go;
on the verge of twisting to turn we rise
to airy and delicate; make shifts of weight;
then dance inside our tubes of clothes;
do movement slivers, improv formations;
so break on through to pounce on up
past bus, car, truck; unweaving gladly,
heads shaken like pebbles from shoes—
till we've moonwalked to some place other;
jinked ankle bells in temples pedestrian;
and wended ways with dervishes whirling.

Matariki from Takarunga, Devonport

Auckland's monster brain, even asleep, pulses
with electric flashes: a live volcanic field—
urban magma, glowing, larval, wormy,
while the Sky Tower blazes like a firebrand to flush
out werewolves, except there's no moon beaming,
just a black vault thick with glitter, celestial
frost wheeling above the summit of Takarunga,
Mount Victoria, eighty-one metres above the harbour;
and I've walked its spiralling road in the dark to keep
a vigil, be a stargazer, a look-out posted in the prow
of a waka, scanning the skies for Matariki's eyes.

I lie on my back against the lip of the crater,
to gaze up like an anti-gravity bungy-jumper
at the star-trek of spaceship Earth in bigger-
than-Imax glory, with 360-degree sensurround;
am gathered into spiral arms of the Milky Way;
then for a moment feel light years from home—
consciously amid the cosmic laboratory a specimen—
and the closed throat of the vent below me hums.
It might be a hangar where raupō kites are stored
that can duel with the hawk, whose cold plumes
coast without lull from Ruapehu or Ngāuruhoe.

Hill leviathan, fit for temple or observatory,
this scoria lump, pitted and terraced, once wore
a cloak woven of fern, bracken, flax, mānuka;
then was a site for palisades, stratagems, ambuscades,
flag-raisings; for signal masts, cannon to warn foes
emphatic as war god Tūmatauenga's stuck-out tongue.
Now I stalk across its carpark a nocturnal weka,

looking towards Rangitoto, Tiritiri, Tīkapa Moana,
below Māui's fishhook, the anchor of the Great Waka,
the moko of some mighty face streaked with stardust—
the wink of tiny eyes sparkling like lures of pāua.

Go tell it on the mountain; let its green bell chime
above cemetery's melancholy, stoplights, roofs.
New tides of day roll in: Te Rā dyes the sea blue,
and floats of a fishing net form islands in the Gulf.
All is flux: shadows boiling; a mad whirl of gulls
chasing ferry's backwash as it departs for Downtown.
Trypot's bubbling anchorage is a cauldron of dolphins
surfacing, or black-shelled mussels steaming in a kitchen.
Curtains go back on a villa window, and a behemoth
glides to the container port like a horizontal skyscraper,
orange as ripe persimmons in winter's leafless orchard.

23 June 2009

The Zero

With a writhe of hands,
this world-famous nobody,
a vacuum really,
an elbow plucker, one of the fans,
casting about for a way to be felt,
makes a once-in-a-lifetime offer
to become frontrunner;
and this unedited emotional genius,
flirtatious pathological liar,
name-dropper, debt-dodger,
silent taunter, foe,
personal confessor,
wreck on the never-never,
Olympian, winner, game-on
whooper punching air,
this hero ready to go—
is then gone.

Lines at Wharf's End

Summer's evening gown ruffles gold silk;
saxophones of stars tilt;
surf ebbs, and beach guitars plink;
conch shells of cloud squeal to pink;

breezes trumpet the sun's farewell;
a flagging cabbage tree rustles its leaves;
night throbs on rusty reefs of roofs;
marimbas of town lights melt towards overseas.

FROM *THE CONCH TRUMPET* (2015)

The Conch Trumpet

Stars are setting westward,
other stars are rising eastward:
a handful of sparks on the horizon,
glow-worms on the roof of a cave.
Scorched grains of colour mask
the reasoning power of the human swarm.
Apparitions in mist, cloaked
or vanished, gone to earth,
emerge in the green heart,
the green lungs of divers.
The blueness of the tongue swells.
The sea chest thumps.
The waka is pelted by ochre dust,
by red pōhutakawa, carried in a waterspout.
A centipede paddles.
Squid wreathe miles of black ink;
scuds of smutty carbon drift.
An iron-sand glaze
is fired by a burning forest.
A hand coils pregnant clay.
Neutrinos oscillate through everything.

Sunday's Song

A tin kettle whistles to the ranges;
dry stalks rustle in quiet field prayer;
bracken spores seed dusk's brown study;
the river pinwheels over its boulders;
stove twigs crackle and race to blaze;
the flame of leaves curls up trembling.
Church bells clang, and sea foam frays;
there's distant stammers of revving engines,
a procession of cars throaty in a cutting,
melody soughing in the windbreak trees,
sheep wandering tracks, bleating alone.
Sunday sings for the soft summer tar;
sings for camellias, fullness of grapes;
sings for geometries of farming fence lines;
sings for the dead in monumental stone;
sings for cloud kites reddened by dusk—
and evening's a hymn, sweet as, sweet as,
carrying its song to streets and suburbs,
carrying its song to pebbles and hay bales,
carrying its song to crushed metal, smashed glass,
and fading in echoes of the old folks' choir.

Raukura

Stone clacks on stone,
so creek lizards slither,
runnels slip through claws,
each cloud's a silver feather.
Mountains flex then soar;
the red tussock pulses.
River's mouth is drowned,
when ocean surges, green
below dark vaulted forest.
The salt spray mist, violet,
granular as dust, climbs
to grasp snow mountains
in fog layers, and above
glides the boat of the moon.

Moriori Dendroglyphs

green tongues lollop round branches
through wounds in bark with deep
affliction like tattoos freshly fingered

surf's blind gravel spat from the sea
rain streaking a small plane's windscreen
as it lands on wind-flattened paddock

black waves of coal an ancient tide
clenched between clay layers
and just them walking in ideation

on limestone walls under kite claws

Trails above Cook Strait

So Farewell Spit, they mocked the seasick;
Tangaroa always gets burnt by the sun.
Bird cries carried by a squall's lick
echo in the ears of Captain Cook,
sunk like an anchor as fathoms break.

Waka creep past wooden islands outrun.
Fish-headed waves snare, skein by skein,
the filigrees of slithery reflection.
Cut those ropes, they said, so the sails can
gather to slowly skywards their way take.

Winged flotillas fly, radiant with lyricism.
Spanked canvas shines in accumulation,
buoyed up by air like honeycombs of foam.
Waves dance in perpetual motion,
stitching the Tasman under swell of moon.

The Hook of Māui

A fanged shank yanks him from open sea.
Silken jellyfish glisten on hot iron-sand.
Mottled green light tattoos a drug-blue gaze.
Stingrays undulate along sunlit nerves.
The road snakes, and cars fishtail in gravel.
His ears are earthenware, glazed by mud.
Gold toetoe rise in hair-triggers from his armpits.
His filaments snarl round a plastic comb.
Police bolt-cutters snag on his tongue stud.
His lungs are stopped with red scoria splinters.
His lips turn black from a summit's pure snows.
His blanket's unbound clay, slid from bedrock.
Night's moths flutter from the cave of his mouth.
He dreams he's woken, wrapped in calm water.

Roadkill

fleece fur feather
petrol fumes
hard rubber wheels
and leather

Syzygy

Moon dreams of moonlight,
cracking sutures of the skull open.
Mouth, moth, o moonlight, flicker.
Dance, moons of May.
Dance, moons of torch-shine.
Moon, tossed over our heads, a ball,
sails towards the net.
Scry the moon, note down marks you see
on her surface reflected in still water.
Moon, round mirror,
veined solid slub, a prism.
A telescope, gibbous grim-moon,
a drinkers' moon—full, fat, cheerfully bright.
Melon moon: pregnant to many moons.
Moon conjuring mystic syzygy,
with the sun in harmony.
Moon's spectral lake, draped weightless
with moonlight, gathering shadow.
Tarot moon, shuffling decks of the zodiac,
leaving runnels of shadow across her forehead.
Knight errant, his black pennant flags hung
on a Golden Holden out in the scrub,
with mattock, shovel and a body,
leaning on the bonnet,
ponders the mellow moon hugely aloft
and crossed by tatters of cloud,
its insignia a kind of stigma.
Moon, her abdomen girdled with stars,
she carries the teardrop of sorrow
tattooed on her cheek.
All the phantom pregnancies sigh and cry.

Once in a blue moon,
everyone grows older, if you need something
to cry on, here's my shoulder,
not cold, but nor does it smoulder.
Hey you, this is the room to chill in,
with its moony glow
of black and blue.
Moon? City lights swallow it,
but there's the neon moon,
and the sizzle of its brand burns till dawn.

Hawk and Butterfly

As the kāhu, a hairline, coasts in clear blue,
yellow gorse stretches under big rock's face,
and barbed wire's strung, enclosing our place.
So we pace at the gates of Te Papa,
made a paradise from haka to haka,
for kiwi by kiwi just passing through,
each carrying a piece of thin silver fern,
cut while you wait from corrugated tin.
Billy's boiling away, down back of beyond;
planed kauri frames a fret-sawn view.
We're listening to the rugby in lemon light,
with a longing for victory, with a dog's sigh.
Rain flutters from horses, skips off a frond,
and forms a sheen on roads in the wet;
till the sun comes out to weakly, and yet
steadily, illuminate the monarch butterfly.

Observatory

Drams of dew shove stars out at dawn.
Dreams of wilding pines stalk tussock fog.
Mountain gowns in pristine satin fold
alcove upon alcove away, to await storms.
Creek music mutters from fiddlehead ferns.
Bees zap lupins; glacier grins at glacier.
Scrubbed-clean scenery hangs its calendar
of lakes at a point in space
where sky's blue crush begins.
The stone sails beneath the sun.

Desirous of mud, of sacks of spuds,
of cows in ranging crowds,
and uncoffined by tumbled outcrops,
earth rises from the roll of scree slopes,
hauls through dry bush in stillness,
feels dusty tyres in revolution,
their makeshift patterns over distance,
then runs on under falling night, satellites,
moons of Saturn seen through a telescope,
dark's singular tumulus of Mount John.

Hydrangeas

Shrubbery's floral bells.
Graceful, and tough as wicker-knots.
Parfait Amour liqueur shots arrayed.
The petalled bathing caps
of synchronised swimmers
in a blue hubbub.
The light opera brigade's charge
in violet rinse clusters
towards the best seats.
Tether of balloons in delicate pinks.
Sleepy heads of nursery beds
cobwebbed with leafy spells.
White wigs of fancy-dress toffs
who lord it over a carnival.
Hazy as clapped chalk dusters
gripped by school monitors.
Bubbly as champagne
in vases on ledges aloft.
The judicial tribunal
risen above a wooden fence.
A bobble of tennis court fans
applauding their own cornucopia
to a garden's very echo.
A razzle-dazzle of pom-poms,
a rave of suburban rah-rah squads.
Hydra-headed and growing more heads,
crouched under masses of cumulus,
colours are your confabulations,
and flowering in that assumption,
you are the crest of the wave.

Nor'wester Flying

Gorse-cutters know they are quids in;
river's pledge is so polished it shines,
as a blind wind gropes the sand dunes.

Cloud whispers brush daylight's ear;
fern question marks form a bush encore;
forlorn heat swings cobbed in webs.

Stone outcrops sideways knock the gale;
grasshoppers thread leaf-storm's blade,
paddocks kick for touch on the tarseal.

Cries of birds interrogate bareback hills
that reveal bleached treatment for bones;
river's harp pings; and music of twig-falls
is blown away by thunder's aerodrome.

River

Begin, spring,
on steep range.
Unfurl fern-scroll,
in light sing,
glance off things,
shimmer by swimmers,
swirl green as willows
stirring tips in summer;
surface under bridges,
while land turns,
to autumn,
where leaves freckle,
winds raise chaff,
dust braids thorns,
hawks hollow the sky,
and warmth creeps
from currents, open
slather for winter
ocean
ever closer.

Summer Rain

Spring trees grow collections of wands,
to conjure gently the colour green,
but in summer drum-taps bounce on water
to ease a tension of the skin,
and when summer rain thunders,
then starts to dance, it is itself the romance,
prancing down the street with silvery feet,
kicking a frou-frou cancan from verandah overhang,
splashing the spatterdashes of an entrance.

Rain brings Fred Astaire's tap-tap across the roof,
before a razz of jazz is given tumultuous applause,
the ozone in the air extinguished like snuff
of golden beeswax melted in candles.
Petulant petals quiver in crimson.
Rain bodies forth a spectacular
earthworm welcome from hitherto undistinguished lawn.

After the storm's glance moves on,
silence fills with birdsong, the sheen of datura,
sky-blue of the violet, whiteness of carnation,
scarlet glow of Iceland poppies—
until the very nectarines blush, as teeth break skin,
grass dries out, heat splits pods,
and all summer breathes from the garden.

Orogenesis

Dug from tiny earth gestures, sometimes a convulsion,
shale fans on the move thaw and freeze: hot then cold.
Frost-heave lifts flakes of rock: ice melts; soil slumps.
Sensors might catch quakes low on the Richter scale
that throw everything up as if off big bull shoulders.
Delicately dancing greywacke seams on tip-toe
contract and flex. Crumbly, bald, boundless strata
bunch and flank, make a pressure graph of fault lines:
axis squeezed between the dialectic of sun and rain.

Some force has left no stone unturned but tumbles
—down climactic slopes steep as speedy escalators—
each to seek true weight on a trial and error basis,
till, caught by river rapids, they bank up as shingle,
and, an eternity later, riverbed dust blown sky-high.

Haast amongst the Moa

Mountains are your eagle claws,
your aquiline beak.
Maverick feathery prey in tussock,
swamp or sandhill,
they were dug from a bog.
Now home is a hollow log
in a museum diorama,
while the billy boils.
The taxidermied crowd regards you
with glass eyes.
Muscular Christians,
whole mustering gangs,
have gone the way of all flesh.
A kea's scream rattles down scree
and up hawk spurs;
a greenstone mere thrills to the marrow.
Wrestling with a taniwha,
on a turbulent riverbed;
eels of water welling from a bore,
as rātā bloom maps the province in red.

Rakaia

Dark feather of the rainbird, riroriro,
sweeps over the ranges, bringing watercolours,
as the facets of ridges ripple with snowmelt,
and each angled rock-face spawns waterfalls,
clear threads woven to join the heart of water
beating in a youthful stampede of spring creeks
that pull apart to bolt through bush; so spiral,
purl, englobe boulders, and jostle back together,
forming a restless racing torrent that collects
brisk water, slow water, slack water, twirligig pools,
ravelling these ribbons and vines into a river strand
descending the mighty spine of the Southern Alps;
and gathering in the flurries of many tributaries,
until the Rakaia springs out of the mountains,
a wily and seasoned campaigner meandering
in lacy loops and twirls through channels,
the gravity of gravels a growl in river's throat:
Rakaia, visible portion of a continuous seepage
pulsing subterranean to the sea, flicking braids,
the gliding pulse of its groundwater going strong.

The Burnt Text of Banks Peninsula

All over Banks Peninsula in the middle of the nineteenth century,
sure-footed on slopes, forest shook out wings;
could not flee; began to singe:
the white cloak was not feathers but smoke—
a hīnaki of creeks twisted and broke.
Axes more weighty than an adze split bark;
tackles harnessed to bullocks dragged logs apart;
peat exposed beneath fallen kahikatea began to rot.
Steam sawmills chugged to life; wairua shrank away:
great trunks of tōtara wallowed down gullies,
stumped up to blades spinning in light and shade,
were cradled so the timber sawn would not warp—
wanted for floors, walls, bridges and wharves.
Wreathes of flames combed gullies to char strewings
and bare blunt brute land: its broken-off stands
reduced to shadows, scars, and a few nīkau palms—
the gallows haze of carbonised trees, intended to purify
and fertilise, hung over paddocks until Gallipoli.

Off the Sheep's Back

Sheep like maggots on a rabbit's tawny pelt …
—Basil Dowling

Sheep crawl on the hill's broad back like swollen slaters
under the stone of the sky …
—Patricia Glensor

I watch the sheep like a pestilence
Pouring over the slopes …
—Denis Glover

Each a crest, each a herald, each emblazoned,
countless on the coat of arms of Victoria's island,
obedient to the virtue of Meekness, hooves on her lap;
the land's black pennant snapping in fierce loyalty:
Meekness, Fidelity, Moderation, then Prosperity.

Tossed-curl cloud: classers fleece cloud that bigs
itself up as sunset in full array—like sewn sacks
stacked to climb for glory in wool stores—or those
risen barred streaks that drift silken, as flocks
crown summits like shocks of snow to the stars.

The fickle trade fair of rag trade's latest collections,
wisps and still more wisps, clipped scanty at first;
not skimped on, skerricks wound-in off jumped-up
merinos: pelt with a heartbeat to snag rosettes and thorns,
before a steel talon rips open the chosen bale of product.

In dustbowl cemeteries of flyblown carcass paddocks,
skeleton thistles and the rabbits' gibbet wire fence,

everything that stinks is holy; Bible's seven-year drought
wavering through bubbled glass of farmhouse windows:
rusted bouquets of ironmongery, car hulks overgrown.

Picturesque classics of ruination, unsettlement,
a Budget black as burnt stubble on a Canterbury run,
black as coal in rail wagons rumbling to Lyttelton;
then a day when shepherds survey the blue horizon
like Prince Aragorn: from the peak of a wool boom.

Old Man Nor'wester

Sometimes Old Man Nor'wester blows, and so exhumes,
amid dust moving, shingle skating, braids shifting,
the rainshadow shape of sheep rustler James McKenzie,
who strolled, dead broke and crook to boot, only to fluke
a landscape he wrapped up tight and carried like a swag,
taking seven-league strides across the Mackenzie country,
preaching sermons in Gaelic to his dog as skinks lay hidden
like shrunken dragons amongst rocks of subalpine basins
furrowed back to basics by that wind; tufts of wool
chasing across the barrel-vault-blue vastness of the sky.

McKenzie, though, vanished beyond lost cairn markers
long ago, his straggly beard legacy of wilding pines,
ragwort, Yorkshire fog, yarrow, gorse, king devil,
mouse-eared hawkweed, a rogues' gallery gathering
in our sanctum sanctorum of ancient lakes and rivers
we will not sandblast back to the past; as powerlines
sough, and scullers row for New Zealand against drag
on Ruataniwha; and rabbits start from bootfalls
in this mirrorland of desires rustled for subdivisions,
hydro-electric dams, boating, the remains of film sets.

Dragonfly wheel energies of Lakes Tekapo, Pūkaki,
Ōhau, the colour of ground-down pounamu, spin
into the Waitaki, as Old Man Nor'wester skips
dynamic water, flicks it over, rippling sunshine's
dismantle of ice into scalding light; until the light
darkens, pent up, or sings seawards, past folded
hills seamed with gullies, farmers' corrugated faces,
electricity snaking north and south, the fizz of life;
and then in the night those gusts trying to prise open
a greenstone door slammed tight on the underworld.

Untold

untold those years that rung as gold
like gold poured from a crucible
the yellow lure of sky ablaze
cracked clay's cliff-edge crumble
flung dust in a stinging haze
perfume stealing good as gold
the song of lilies lupins sunshowers
gold in kōwhai gorse mānuka
gold of root hairs that climb from mud
gold of fern sap bubbled from ponga
gold underpinnings in a cloud-span
gold's beaten froth that scuds to land
gold bell-chimes of quarter-hours

gold's branch upon branch in rivers
gold in bird feathers mottled salt
gold spills of tobacco leaf makings
gold unreeled and flaked or chipped
gold the twig the nest the thread
gold the stump the nub the chunk
gold the skin the light's gleams pulsing
gold splinters dyes scourings
gold a broken-handled axehead
that only yesterday it seems
split the felled tōtara trunk
for five hundred fenceposts
and an old man's coffin

The Visitation

McKenzie kneels near Waitaki,
enters a tree poem in a log-book.
Seals it up with highway tar,
hammering leaf against leaf.
Mountains echo his amphitheatre.
Raindrops pluck skins on Pūkaki.

Ignoring creek splutter, rain's tangi,
stump by stump arrivals advance
across the Devil's Half-Acres
to massacres of feathery kiwi.
As one of that kidney Hātana knew,
McKenzie loosens his necktie for a dance.

In his gunny sack he clutches harpoon heads,
gathers pounamu blades from iwi.
Lantern flames shadowbox the canvas,
and flittering shoals of galaxiids
fall in stars over whaleboat shapes,
silent waka anchored, silhouetted.

Daybreak the colour of rosehips, McKenzie
climbs from Rākaihautū's footprint,
clings to bowsprit of the windjammer pitched
on the big top of a spinning nor'wester—
with a spyglass of islands crooked in his arm,
and all the ocean before him.

Atua of Nowhere Zen

Elders photographed staring at gold-rush sun
could not see daylight through a Union Jack,
or rabbit after rabbit bolt from the gun.

Kids in cotton smocks made sing-song;
mustered for Anzac biscuits, gathering
blue-gum leaves to blow a cheery tune on.

Merino jumpers were strung along
the wee gully; with father out fencing,
a slip of a girl tackled the flock alone.

Hail ploughed its block of despond;
thickened a Captain Cooker's hairy back;
encased a sod hut; flattened a fern frond.

The far volcano's catapulted boulder
dropped from dug-up sky like a hot scone
to land smack on Lake Taupō's kisser.

Tuatara crawled to the swimming snow
of bridal-veil falls, that had such a glow
as worms had prophesied, under Waitomo;

but hiding out like a bush-ranger's grave is
the spot where all rainforest goes to rack,
and only the caterpillar remembers this.

The historic places turn towards a dream
while necklaces of votive whalebone, worn
by astronauts of inner space, gleam.

Clouds sail sweet bouffant flotillas;
possums stew; sheep cook by the book;
a godstick spells tales of grandmothers.

The tour guide buzzes, like a fly, stuck
in the marmalade of bitter autumn
varnishing all the hills of Nowhere Zen.

Erewhon Unearthed

Skies run, streaked bloody like fleeces shorn.
Strainers twang symphonies in milk and gold.

Empire Rose and *Sun Boy* sail on the tide.
Daisies nod from spring paddocks, stirred.

Tussock's sunbaked pelt jumps and rolls.
Sugar spoons rattle with tea-shop's prattle.

The moa's calcified rugby ball shines,
plucked from scrums of muddy leg-bones.

Hail pings grave bell-jars in sad chimes;
the snick of tiny hail counts baby teeth,

as tree stumps whiten along Dead Horse Row.
Corsets rip, stripped back to whalebone cages.

Found tremors unearth time's brass-bound capsule.
Wings glow amber inside kauri gum's weight.

Glass arcades surface from submarine depths.
Going for a skate, with beer belly bounce,

truckloads of grey silt are chucked up high.
Cashmere Hills cardigans, faded to pink,

shrink in the wash of a bushwhacked laundry.
The smell of money leaves the oily rag,

tossed by whole-earth mechanics.
Coin's flipped downside promotes a fire sale.

Heretics get stuck in with a mixed hot grill.
Bats climb, freed by the great snail's betrayal.

Colonel Shag's cliff-face cormorants preen,
while zephyrs ride, teased by sailboard teens.

Beacon

The glow-worm says, let there be light.
Axes bold as love strike for the heartwood.
The kauri table remembers the forest,
and the conch shell calls to the sea.
Through a candy shimmer the waves
on shore open their summer novels.
Crickets' midday curriculum goes scritch-scritch.
Kazoos, comb-and-paper, and harmonica
begin the bee and wasp summer orchestra.
An orchestration of herds, too, undulant
as tentacles and flowing like a lowing river.
Stones rattle backwards at Trotters Gorge.
Lake salmon leap in silver-blue plumage.
Four-wheel vortex, chipmunk techno, bleeps at sunset.
A possum growls, another howls, a third coughs.
Fugitive shadows steal across the moon.
Pebble-mouthed creeks lisp wicked to night stars.
Emerson's 'Bookbinder', cold as an eel's nose.

Sound and Fury

Not stony silence in Kiwi backblocks,
but quiet rustling of ferrets and stoats,
the blether of sheep, the blither of wind,
road gangs scraping shovels in two-four time.
Bang, bang of settlers throwing up a house;
diggers, back and forth, toss screwball yarns.
Stockwhips crack and bullockies curse;
a steam train crosses sixty-five bridges.
Old-guard swan-song, hee-haw of Bonassus;
while Bob Semple crowed as he rode the land,
it seems he failed to catch the Royal Ear.
Magpies' quardle-oodle-ardle-wardle
heard as cat-bell and dog-whistle remix;
motorvating truck drivers ditto that uptick.
Bogans, cashed up, await gentrification,
seeking a personal tutor in Enzed Lit.
Skim and Scam, borne by budget jet,
arrive from Greece to fleece supermarket flocks.
A crusader caped in silver fern flag
conjures Anzackery from an army surplus bag.
The gurgle of a politician's liquored voice signs
uncashable cheques in front of cameras
with the silver plume of a heron feather.
White-gold pipelines chugging towards town,
irrigator stutter sucking the well-bore dry,
bring the sound and fury of moo-moo land.
Hear the hoofbeats of stampeding herds;
be last man standing in a rolling maul;
and from deep depression in the Tasman Sea,
be rescued by blood of the underdone lamb.

2015 New Zild Book Awards Considered as a Five-Horse Race

They're off and racing now, a boxed set
at first, away fairly well down the straight.
And it's open slather, as the front three break
loose from Holus Bolus and Hoi Polloi,
already struggling to keep up
with the favourites. Giddy Goat's
book of poetry is parked on the outside,
as Chomping Chum's novel leads,
followed by How's Yer Father's
biography. Yes, Chomping Chum's
the leader now, by a length from Holus Bolus
and the rest … here comes Chomping Chum,
coming home great guns. No, Giddy Goat's
scampered clear, followed by How's Yer Father.
Giddy Goat and How's Yer Father neck and neck,
but wait it's Chomping Chum through the middle,
scattering the dirt, getting her head just past the post,
by a nostril, by a toothbite. Just pips How's Yer Father
being gored by Giddy Goat, Chomping Chum is champion!

Ode to Coffee

for Larry Matthews

Even from the first sip,
carousels of whirling cups start up,
and that rollercoaster loop-the-loop
Haunted Mansion fluttery bats feeling,
that Fun Mountain Climb blue ceiling sensation,
that whinny of hoof beats across the heart,
that giddy sugar-shock hit as neon flashes
and you float through hysteric glamour on the liquid mean.
So here's the thing, the molecular throwdown,
whether a skinny on a leash,
or a power mango latte in a grease-
trap, or a double-decaf with almonds to set
yourself up for a mega-mall go-around—
though light years away from the caramel-
coloured hard-sell of industrial flavours and Planet
Heartburn's 'tree-fresh' OJ—
whether black for the red-eye, the jet-lag,
black for the loved-up, black even unto those that gag
at bitter crystallisation of seething wells,
and each drop a silky piano note
steamed from the roasted bean,
cupped in cardboard, polystyrene,
painted glass, or hand-thrown ceramic,
and summoning up wavering syrups of Araby,
wraiths of Colombian mojo elixir,
haloes of Ethiopian mist, earth spices,
java jive, Papuan sing-sing,
or atomic Afro's joyous-bubbled woosh,
here's the thing: had you the ability

to read those grounds, you might see
that the concept, let this be
your commodity fetish,
has ever schemed
its slo-mo assumption
of your taste-buds,
even from the first sip.

Freedom Songs of the Vietcong

John Doe spoke from our back porch in sixty-six,
in bad tones, to channel Victor Hugo at fever pitch.
'I may not make old bones,' said he—
as Eight Immortals were crossing the sea—
'but I know that wherever I may roam'—
and he cupped his hands like a megaphone,
his face desolate, his tears sprung on cue—
'I'll seek the Gate of Luminous Virtue.'

A Ravi Shankar raga played on the stereo,
I see him there still, though it was years ago,
picked out in darkness by fluoroglare,
a wide-eyed Polaroid with shaggy hair,
teeth tubes humming like a tuning fork,
tripping on a tab of Windowpane's torque,
Over Mekong's Delta droned bomber planes,
black smoke from rice paddies reflected flames.

Dust devils rose in those golden summers,
to the clang of the 13th Floor Elevators,
Moby Grape rock, Strawberry Alarm Clock,
to groovy vinyl go-go boots on the hop.
Ho Chi Minh's trail of gardens lay concealed,
filaments from silkworm cocoons unreeled,
dragon clouds grew from a napalmed bodhi tree.
Newsreels showed monks burning for liberty,
as John Doe undid the name tag from his big toe,
and danced to 'Barbara Ann' in our family bungalow.

Night Shades

They turn, and you see a tip of flame
reflected from the lighter up close,
each eye bracketed by a frame,
face pinned in place by shades,
little boxes to house the gaze—
walled-in space, viewless vision.
They might punch your lights out.
Future's in shades, black on black,
a cosmic zenith of rock star glitz,
or else zilch of shadowed tribunals,
funerals for the null and void,
cameras for denizens in zoos.

They turn, so you see a tip of flame
reflected from the lighter up close,
and caught light orbits each frame,
as if the opaque lenses are a question,
or a questioner inside the haze
of the question posed by that razor
glitter of obsidian, its closure
and erasure. Eye seeking eye—
a goo-goo eye, a terror eye,
a zero eye, a tranced eye,
a pinned eye, a wheeling eye,
the blank eyeless staring abyss.

The Death of Gaddafi

We perch in our eyries looking on,
ripened and rotting,
some with a migraine
seething like maggots in the brain,
other with thoughts like abscesses pus-filled,
that maybe this is art hanging from a gibbet,
castrated by carnivorous birds,
or bloody as a movie's bullet ballet,
while voices of the great unwashed
rise to vapour trails,
and junoesque jezebels—
jacuzzi jazz babies clad
in a job lot of global oddments—sling Kalashnikovs
to jab at compulsive tourists in arresting scenes,
and at those souvenir hunters who reminisce
through the twentieth century's auction rooms
with throat-clutching sentiment.

So he crept doubtful and twitching
down the dark interstices of pipes,
emerging between the grout and nubble,
where the hissing hesitancy of anticipation alarmed him,
and he collapsed in a nearby drain
where everything was kind of run-down
and second-rate, yet where also something
had teasingly begun to take shape,
a mirage of dust and shadows,
spelling the living end,
and smelling of petroleum as sun-up arrived
with the whomp whomp of rockets.

So tank salvoes wreck chrome logos,
where flashpoints flare, sunguns glare
and camera lenses blur the air—
thus the naked capitalist
with his cheesy soaps, his reversible bandannas,
his gold-plated pistol, does not, after all,
glide into the witness protection programme
with a sneer, but dies in a waking nightmare.

Glory be to rogue states and stateless rogues,
the convoys of exiles at home nowhere,
and driving from country to country,
as from their keys dangle shrunken heads—
so the story is told by his and hers newsreaders
who make a toothsome twosome,
and told by clique versus claque versus cabal,
and told by fame-machine journos phoning in the performance,
in anonymous international airport idiom
from non-publicity-shy trouble-spots,
which are in a steady state of surface tension,
a steady state of glory be, glory be,
that serves as entertainment for the grounded
waiting by the conveyor belts for their ship to come in.

The neon tigers of the new democracy
splish-splash through blood money;
abetted by a smarmy army of media savants
in a sticky part of the globe leaking oil,
with all the moral cachet of a shampoo sachet.

So here's to a non-recognition of the nameless,
to the permanent maladjustment
that will never reanimate the depersonalised,

as the mob bolts, parcelling out angst,
frenetic plastic, bales of cash, bank bonfires.
His death is an opera, a narcosis, a new religion
to inflame the veins,
and become lightning flashes
deep inside the brainstorms of his tribe.
His fluff has been napalmed off,
and fed to chimneys, to smokestacks of rumour mills,
by a crowd of animated gargoyles
coming off a hit, a fix;
and scunge has left its high tide mark on him,
as if he had been doped to his dead eyeballs,
to the golden bullet points
of his stabbed corpse presentation,
the four hundred thousand blows of ill-feeling
addressed to his legacy;
for democracy is the burn-off of body fat,
democracy is a Coke robot on every street corner,
democracy is the look of the outlaw
on the face of the consumer,
and the sound of branded chains talking crappuccino,
for these are the last days of general rhetoric,
before the platforms are vacated,
and the knowing bodies buried
under the jargon of obsolescence,
leaving only a fragrance of sweatshop.

Testament of Databody Dave

Hello, Databody Dave here—what am I but
a collection of information items subject to panoptic
tracking and Cloud control: the eternal sunshine
of the spotless mind? Am I interrogating the system,

or is the system interrogating me for a predictive
Wikipedia of the self? What I Know Is just a search
for a signal in the noise, joining the typing arms
race of eager communicators. Once were a nation

of conspicuously absent consumption, where everything
happened behind closed doors; now we've thrown the house wide
to open-plan indoor-outdoor flow, barbecue pits
and its own Facebook page, as doddery old

diddy men, knowing diddly-squat about anything
anymore, join the young net surfers who only know
on a need to know basis, otherwise content to chew gum
and post skateboard near-misses, as their earbud iPod fizzes.

Facebook, what is that but electronic galley slaves
furiously pounding keyboards to row their boat forward,
making users strike-targets for predatory sales teams,
trapped in a status-sphere of cool apps and stale pap

as technocapitalism's endless ooh and aah soundtrack
forms an unbreakable compact to provide finer
and finer tweaking of social networking via avatars,
substitutes and personalised kilos of sugar?

Outpourings as unstoppable as the Huka Falls:
tiddlywinkers with tapered fingers twiddle
out texts and Twitter tweets, stripping a topic bare—
locusts moving on, having appropriated, eviscerated,

and marketed yesterday's news as a must-have,
must-see version of same old same old echo chambers
of like-minded sharers maintaining vigils of the vigilant
and threads of the dead on behalf of opinion research agencies.

They get up your nose with their fibre-optic hose,
their cold calls offering flim-flam to confuse.
You will know them by their rhubarb, rhubarb, rhubarb,
those gurus selling spiritual values in soluble capsule form

with talk of naked society, surveillance society,
franchise society, atomised society, sedated society,
but if you look round to blame someone, no one's
there, just algorithms taking care of business.

Six billion's a crowd, but seven billion's crowd-sourcing,
with givers, takers, window-lickers in cyberspace,
and ambulance-chasers assembled in the distance,
as green actors attempt to offer some resistance

to an anarchic world of pass-the-parcel debt,
shadow banks, vulture capitalists, Milton Friedman,
the glub-glub of boat people pushed under by boat
shoes of the best-performing banksters in Oz.

I'm so over it, the over-easy, over-familiar,
over-consumed, slack-jawed, over-done, over-run-
by-cruise-ship, big-bang boomer mentality:
all one heaving packing case of banjaxed bollocks.

Fatigued hipster seeks hipster replacement therapy:
escape from the knowing winking calculating flattery;
the quantative easing for the squee and the twee;
yet another colloquy of sippers and garglers

fumigating their bridgework with finest pinot noir,
furtively consulting phones for inflammatory spam
in the mirrorball gleams of a casino beano,
while battlers grope for change on their knees outside.

I'm drinking decaf in the global warming.
I'm hunched over a gasper in the global ageing.
I'm perched on a push-bike in high-visibility vest,
and updating my status: hashtag hand-jiving
high-fiving, bumping-booty, total-retro frug-fest.

THREE POEMS FROM *SNAP* (2017)

I
With Woven Mats

With woven mats
my muse's bedroom
is an albatross nest,
where she contemplates
the moons of her nails.

II
Love Bite

She fills his heaven,
rocks his world,
oils his wheels—
then shoves him under …

III
Dog

The family pet that runs away,
returns home,
and coughs up human fingers.

FROM *EDGELAND* (2018)

Edgeland

Awks: you winged Auk-thing, awkward, huddling;
you wraparound, myriad, amphibious,
stretchy, try-hard, Polywoodish
juggernaut; you futurescape, insectivorous,
Ākarana, Aukalani, Jafaville, O for Awesome,
still with the land-fever of a frontier town—

your surveyors who tick location, location, location,
your land-sharks, your swamp-lawyers, your merchant kings,
your real-estate agents who bush-bash for true north,
your architecture that fell off the back of a truck,
your shoebox storerooms of apartment blocks,
your subdivisions sticky as pick and mix lollies;
you fat-bellied hybrid with your anorexic anxieties,
your hyperbole and bulimia, your tear-down and throw-up,
the sands of your hourglass always replenished,
your self-harm always rejuvenated, unstoppable;
you binge-drinker, pre-loader, storm-chaser,
mana-muncher, hui-hopper, waka-jumper,

light opera queen, the nation's greatest carnivore;
cloud-city of the South Pacific, it's you the lights adore.

Flying In, Southside

At Māngere the airport welcomes you to Middle Earth,
coasting on a jet's wing and a karakia,
but the industrial parkland unfolds as generic,
though 'nesian mystics harmonise snatches of melody
on Bader Drive by the fale-style churches of Little Tonga,
all the way round the Town Centre to busy PAK'nSAVE,
from whose carpark the Mountain looks back, submerging.

Manaia sail across blue heaven to catch daydreams;
they glide like slo-mo fa`afafine above South Auckland:
the big box stores, all in orange green yellow or red,
as big as aircraft hangars in this polycotton lavalava
wraparound hibiscus paradise of Pap'toe,'Tara, Otahu'—
the Happy Coin marts, the fly-by-night clearance outlets,
the stack 'em high, sell 'em cheap, plastic whatnot bins.

A pearl nacre overcasts closed abattoirs of Southdown,
colonial headquarters of Hellaby's meat empire,
shunting yards of Ōtāhuhu Railway Workshops.
Two-dollar leis sway outside shops on Great South Road.
There's Fiji-style goat curry and Bollywood on screens,
kava, taro, fish heads on ice, hands of green bananas—
no sign of Sigatoka blight amid tart tangelo pyramids.

The suburban origami of bungalow roofs is folded over,
under the warmth of 'Māngere'/'lazy wind': so hot and slow
it barely moves the washing on thousands of clotheslines.
Planes touch down; sirens yammer through the tailbacks;
Macca's golden arches sweat the small hours,
and a police chopper after midnight bugs the sky;
weaving back and forth over quiet streets of Manurewa.

King Tide, Northside

The moon is close, at her perigee, imperious,
summoning the salty fever of a king tide.
Volcanoes seem to change position,
to drift further out, or drift closer;
and creeks are frothy-mouthed.
What's salvaged from ocean
might splash up on shore,
ferried from creaking timbers anchored well out,
gilding what it covets with a kia ora tātou,
and a good sousing for whatever can be caught.
Tank Farm to Silo Park, they are keeping
their heads up, though boardwalks are lapped.
Paddlers frolic; sand flaunts its wet silks.
Crowds are shoaling like īnanga.
The king tide purls on Meola Reef pathway,
and makes a long grab for East Coast Bays,
The king tide casts a net for gasping creatures,
for reclamation of the waterfront,
for the holy scallop of sand in every blessed cove,
knowing that if you cut a thousand-metre channel
between Ōtāhuhu Creek and the Manukau Harbour
you could create Aotearoa's third-largest island
to ebb around, searching for wetlands.
And Auckland's flapping like a kahawai,
flapping greeny-blue and silvery,
above all the speckled cockled shelly beaches,
as long-legged girls walk by the creep of the tide,
and the biceps of blokes bulge, hefting a rugby ball.
Pōhutakawa know the king tide well;
they cliff-hang like trapeze artists,
branches parallel to the ground

and demanding elbow room.
They have a ring-side seat.
At night, the old soak of the sea
will go rolling rolling rolling home,
dark beneath the phosphorescence of the city.

Hauraki

Dark as flax cloaks stained with ash is the isthmus.
Fast thunderheads dim the evershifting light's pulse.
A howly bag of weeping winds and drunkard gusts
hurries in from Hauraki Gulf to empty holus-bolus
rain squalls from Kawau Island to the Hūnuas.
First dull spit, then steady spots, then drops in surplus.
Hinewai's the light rain, Te Ihorangi the monsoon colussus—
in crescendo, like Pasifika drummers felt in the solar plexus.
Dragging their sousing trains, the holy rains process.
Dog bowls runneth over; quick-time car wipers make a fuss.
Pavements are eel alleys; roads are wheke tentacles—
they fling out and grip as suckers of a great octopus.
Rain prods earthworms in darkness to rise from humus,
emerging on Eden Park's turf to writhe exultant, tremulous.

Two Takes on the Waitākere Ranges

The hills and mountains are covered in wood and
every valley has a rivulet of water.
—Captain James Cook, 1773

I

Te Waonui-a-Tiriwa, awesome forest of Tiriwa,
with fantails darting up, waterfalls jinking down,
with skinks sidling beneath green mingimingi,
and arcades of fern dropping giddily to the sea:
falling to the tossing white manes of the toetoe,
or rising to rātā's glowing cloak of carmine.
The hollow pūriri are catacombs, and dead fronds
cling to tree ferns like feathery brown ballgowns.
Deep in gullies, the mānuka is dry, or damp.
Down such a gulch, the last stand was made:
Mahuika's fingernails smouldered, forest crackled.
Charcoal makers admired their handiwork:
a scarred, charred phoenix awaiting rebirth
as mānuka scrubland, exotic shrubs, stoat habitat.

II

Early in the morning, they propped up the stars:
hammered bronze bark stroked by sunlight,
their heartwood a greeny-yellow or light gold,
great cylinders proud to the sky, their crowns
of orchids and moss, cities for aphids, beetles, spiders.
They flourished as the taproots of the citadel: kauri.
Those Samsons of timber barons pulled them in,
pillars of the temple, working out the resource,
chapter and verse, chiselled, adzed, milled, rolled;
cradled on wheels of the bush sawyers' railway

to crash, beached, foundered, to be lifted
and dumped without ceremony in a scow,
or rafted, floated, towed en masse to Onehunga
and a fate as flooring, cupboards, desks.

The Sleepers

They named the forty-eight sleepers
with names that enshrined imperial purpose,
from Mount Hobson to Mount Victoria,
and made them triumphal arches fallen,
taken away one truckload at a time, so that,
led by the hand, landscape knuckled under
to dirt worked over for foundations of a town.
Governor Grey endowed them as domains,
as 'Mountains' or 'Kings'; and for the pioneers
volcanoes were navigational beacons, but soon
that archipelago, rising from a sea of roofs,
was hollowed, and even levelled. Mounts
Albert and Smart and Wiri Mountain
were shifted beneath the Main Trunk Line
as ballast between Whangārei and Ohakune,
or later dumped under the motorway causeway
across the upper harbour. Nothing remains of Ōtara Hill.
Puketutu Island was flattened, pink scoria taken
for Māngere runways, for Jean Batten's aerodrome.
Villages were brought closer to Queen Street,
and each other, by dynamited volcanic rubble
crushed for a base layer of basalt chips over
a sub-base of aggregate—all topped with tarseal.
Concrete pavements and asphalt footpaths
sat on steamrollered clinker, blistered with bubbles.
They built from blue stone the prison, street kerbs,
barracks, wall boundaries, the police station.
They knocked down timber, built up in basalt.
At the quarry face were gravel-shovelling champions.
Lava flow, gorges ghostly with rain vapour,
became bitumen skeins, tying the suburbs.

Of those forty-eight sleepers, half are gone,
or nearly gone; only Rangitoto has stayed untouched.

Lake Wakatipu

A jade lizard bends in a circle,
chasing its tail;
straightens, and darts for a crevice.
Mist swathes in grey silk the lake:
flat-stomached, calm, slow-pulsed,
a seamless bulk.
Vapours spiral,
pushing up to a cloud-piercer,
where snow has been sprinkled
like powder from a talc can at height.
Grandeur stands muffled.
The *Earnslaw* headbutts shorewards.
After lying prone for years,
rocks shift downwards
at speed, eager to wheel
through air, crash in a gully,
and not move.
The lake buttons up to dive deep,
leaving a perfectly blank black space,
through which you might fall forever.

Distant Ophir

I went looking for the nightingale,
for the rose, and found corrugated iron,
scent of wild thyme, cry of a hawk.

I felt a breeze lift in the orchard,
to waken the leaves from slumber
and entangle memories in apricot heat.

Monday was washday, Tuesday ironing,
Wednesday cleaning, Thursday baking,
Friday shopping, Saturday sports games.

Sunday meant church, promise of roast dinner.
Air stood dry and warm beneath pine trees.
Crickets leapt over sunflower radiance.

Summer's elixirs glistened in green jelly.
Jam was given in peach and cherry.
Quicksilver sank in the foxed mirror.

The breeze, a stir of quiet fingers,
plucked at floury puffs of petals,
fluffed sponge cake, buttered big scones.

Furniture stacked, empty windows blank,
fine bones showing, faded curtains folded,
the farmhouse went for a knockdown price.

If I peer hard now through the late afternoon,
I can almost see as far as distant Ophir,
and cargo from Otago, raising the dust.

Southern Embroidery

A killjoy's claw, a feathered dawn,
the liar's tripwire that traps birdsong;
the kāhu's lunge, a car's speed,
magnetic mountains burning white.
Turquoise lake; skeletal rock clack
to sound the glooms of algal blooms,
freak-out traverse, funky forest floor,
blood-hot springs and hail's cool millions.
A rainbow sifts gravel for colour.
Rusty prayer wheels of seagulls turn.
The whale's maw pulls everything in,
while octopus tentacles with motion seek
sudden fanfares of dolphin whistles.
Sooty shearwater flocks crowd the sky:
drawn black thread, thicker and thicker.
On a single breath float moon and feather.

Game

Mud-cracked, mud-punked, mud-brindled,
each foot unplugged from montane bogs,

they are tackled in mud, and then some,
strugglers sliding to the splash of try line.

They catch the future, turn it over in their hands;
then down they scrum, with mud-flecked faces.

Again they fall, as if thrown to the very bottom,
held down in the muddy slither of trenches.

Climbing up again through troughs of rain,
they are the whole earth, kicking for touch.

Spinners

Marsh grasses flap like a magic carpet,
ready to fly; ripples crank across water;
lifted seeds, skerricks, beetle husks, ping.
The bracken's eiderdown floats.
Punished hair farmers thumb a ride,
with sheaves of pummelled tussock.
Slow white blades chop at airy nothing.

Weather loosens stones on a hill.
A townie, I drift by tarn and lichen,
pitched up on a rock parabola,
as turbines below lift angelic wings
and a cogwheel momentum turns
its zap-zap revolution to tame hurly
burly, a quickening when isobars tighten.

Bone blade, shadow stalker, skylark trill,
a hawk soars to let fall a feathered kill.
In wind's eye, a child's windmill on a stick
hangs motionless till flippers fiercely flick.
The dervishes whirl their arms in bedlam:
giant spirits droning lung-burst stanzas,
prayer hum blown away in electric bonanzas.

The Wilder Years

Us, with our sewing, quilting, plumbing bees,
going hard yakker till the eleventh hour,
we'll be throwing on the barbie one more sacred cow,
and tossing the hoons mallowpuffs and macaroons
to keep them bemused between beers,
then hosing it all down with tanker milk.
A clinking canticle of glasses is poured
as all Kiwiland gets on board—
in sheep's clothing looking wolfish, a teeth-gnashing nation.

These shaky isles of geyserland porridge,
wind gusts and snow, and blinding sunshine
spread like butter on the bread of the mundane,
show all the blue, blue days of shunted livestock
are otherwise fine, so get in behind, ya mongrels.
You can, in this country, walk on water,
so long as you don't rock the boat,
but always speak the truth and always shut the gate.

How we yearn to be lost and found on shores
of islands loveliest, loneliest, fierce and raw,
though often rent asunder by thud and blunder,
and sometimes by pillage and plunder,
running down the mountainous spine,
where greenstone's a hollow pampered jade,
and pounamu jiggles on a piece of string.
Flag, anthem, dairy herd, rugby team identity
are carried on the narrow back of the new Hawaiki,
to the jeers of old-time mountaineers
whose core-sample memories are all that remain
of a rattletrap past wrapped in its own bombast,
its own jars of extract of sticky black yeast.

Twice branded by the slash-mark of Zorro,
Enzed is machine washable and in a state of global warming.
Enzed is delirium tremens, too, a trigger warning.
Enzed is a mega uplift junket, a berm with a view,
a watchamacallit, Lotto prize, gold-plated thrill,
a hoiho five-spot, mohua hundie, kārearea kill,
a folding koha, whio blue duck, ten-dollar bill.

Kettle

Gumboot, smoky gunpowder,
dried tea that grew
on rich, warm earth.

In kitchen's dawn gleam,
tea at the still point
of a turning world.

For snuggled bedfellows,
estranged by dreams,
tea leaves darken hot water
to the very end of steam.

Over cups of tea, we peer
at morning's blackened toast.

Poured cups of tea, sympathetic
vibrations of a heart to heart.

His forehead shines,
a polished teapot:
he's making tea,
amid crusty sauce bottles.

A storm brews
in the chink of china mug,
the tinkles of a teaspoon.

On a rainy afternoon,
she's marooned,
with a packet of macaroons,
and endless cups of tea.

In the last tea-room in town,
conversations about tea stains;
stale cake crumbs on doilies.

Teetotallers are slurping
through ancient dentures,
back when tea was tuppence,
served in Crown Lynn cups.

A cup of tea on the deck,
a cup of tea on the run,
a cup of tea in the past.

New Year's Day at Byron Bay

I'm older now at Byron Bay,
rediscovering its tourist schemes,
while clarity pours from crest to crest,
serenely leading the chasing wash.
The summer crowd loves the whoosh.
It bobbles wet-backed till it gleams,
sunk thigh-deep in the seethe of New Year's Day,
holy for Australians and the Kiwi,
rising drenched from crystal glow,
a roll-on spiced, jasmine, sunblock gloss,
as the human wrack shimmers away
to a haze of sea-meadow,
where sharks cruise like midget submarines.

In starry Jesus hair streams,
a goofy-foot walks a water-quake.
A foaming breaker drapes his shoulder.
He flips upside-down through a mirror,
then kicks for the blue light,
kicks to where the rip curl lifts
over his ears its redeemer's shower.
The ocean glitter's a soft icing, his board planes,
and blue his cloud-swallowing dreams,
bound in foamy loops, whisked to gold's height
for a sponge cake the sun might bake,
He's the jackpot casino winner who preens.
Kids pound the waves with their fists.

In Byron, the anointed test the sunbeams.
Above swamps where crocodiles lurk,
car engines idle, waiting for fossil fuel.
Heat sneaks in and fingers everything,
making greasy marks, while I watch
from a pricey beer balcony
the hippy bus going to Nimbin,
and poolside aquacade teams,
and shoppers whose branded backpacks
hold the globe. Motorists fume
in traffic serpents at the roundabouts.
Their cars growl, having drunk truth serum.
Tourists raise their melting ice-creams.

Spidermoon

The spidermoon burns
reddish-yellow yolky;
sleepwalking through night fields,
a spinner's tranced orb.
Trapezes drift on silk bolas.
Strands carry them a long way
to spokes, sticky spirals,
guyed trapdoors.
Wakefulness in shadows at dawn;
soft, quivering snuffle of a muzzle,
nosing grass and bat urine:
the dog's off the chain.

The bombora of Mount Chincogan
tips a green wave down to the yoga church,
and the amped-up ukulele player,
who busks for coins outside the IGA
with 'Yes, We Have No Bananas'.
The check-out chick pops her bubblegum.
Lorikeets squabble beyond the library.
A parrot-man coaxes;
his shoulders are perches.
A galah oohs and aahs.
He feeds the bird clinging to him.
The flock beats wings to a harbouring.

Summer kneads trees
the colour of a bloodnut hamadryad.
Sunflowers glow more yellow
than fluffy sponge cake.
Cicadas swing like pendant earrings.

Grasshoppers from fallen clothes pegs leap.
Brush turkeys stalk a picnic sandwich.
Tiny lizards pause, scuttle, pause.
A goanna hotfoots it
over the brickwork of the barbie.
Hot tin roofs
make with their creaking cha-cha.

The air's dry as a dog biscuit.
Stones clang under dusty cars.
The burning tar sports a shiner.
A water dragon's clean-bowled,
spread across the road.
The bat some kid shot at
hangs by claws from a wire.
Birds twitter, rayed out
against the phone transmitter.
The sun's hard-boiled in its shell.
A spinnaker of cloud gets the wind up,
and bolts for the wild blue yonder.

Moreton Bay

When it's stinking hot at twelve o'clock,
earthy aromas rise and vent.
Something's conjured in a gutbucket
and tossed bloodily in a wok
to quarrel with a guzzle of noodles.
Somewhere, someone faces the chop,
gets the elbow, and, down in the mouth,
thumbs the nose like a clothes peg.
The pineapple factory clanks;
a rock melon's guts ferment,
spilled on grease-trap spikes.
Op-shop fabrics swelter.
Crow's caw lays down the law.
Fibrolite freedoms let draughts in.
A tin roof's holed like a colander,
shotgunned with sun's dust.
Shacktown's galvanised iron creaks
beneath clatter of fangs, claws, beaks.
Pelicans roost on rusty bridge posts.
Moreton Bay fig trees engage
in elephantine creep.
Against crinkle-eyed seawater,
freckled knuckles row a dinghy out.
Still as a lizard, a man fishes
at evening for a plume of white stars
to answer the day's long thirst.

Heat

Heat wears the head of a kangaroo,
a scarred leather apron with a pouch.
Heat shrink-wraps blood, guts and glory
into the stew of a tossed-out meat pack,
on which a live fur of fungus sprouts.
Heat reveals testimony, and unpeels
insect scribbles of a paperbark story.
Heat clangs a rusted-up tap dead.
Heat tastes eucalyptus on the wind.
Heat stuffs the rump of the outback
into a slow cooker from a gunny sack.
Heat dries plumage to desert sand.
Heat throws a dry-course curse
on mongrel margins, and worse.
Heat puts a stop to green leaf-claws.
Heat places a frog's song on the slide.
Heat causes a koala's clutch to contract.
Heat bends metal to sword-blades,
slashing zeros and zeds on rusted hulls.
Heat lets ashes of forest offerings
settle on towels along the beaches.
Heat wobbles the whole seaboard.
Heat sends the shimmer of a jogger
to bound away like a kangaroo,
from road stoplights stuck on red,
in search of rain's cool wherewithal.

In Crematoria

My cyclone unearths a sacred larrikin.
My boom water stagnates in beer can ziggurats.
My book of scribbly gum opens on firebombs.
My mill of ants seethes like a frenzied caliphate.
My cracked glass smokes out a season of arsonists.
My Yellow Monday crackles with payback's clamour.
My blank TV screen, black as celebrity shades,
concentrates its gleams and waits for recognition:
the spontaneous ignition of daytime soaps.
My true horizon dances on blowtorched grasses.
My dry storm bursts out of the slammer,
to swing down like jailbait from a lightning tree.
My scrub explodes on high beams of heat,
white as; other colours burn to electricity.

Panel Beater

A high-maintenance, G20 Sky Father.
A desalinised, compostable, home-birther.
A granular plastic skin with vents and grafts.
A bug-eyed and hernia-sprung wobble-board.
A gall wasp, sawfly, slug and aphid display shield.
An age-hardened, unleavened, half-eaten spiced bun.
An earworm filthy as Lord Melbourne's waistcoat.
A great wombat the colour of tainted coffee-whitener.
A large bowel collider facing early-onset nothingness.
A heavy metal bombardment of daylight bulbs.
A Day of Penitence, factory-farmed, tooter the sweeter.
A camouflaged, eye-patched god-shaped hole.
A whack-a-mole clay and burnt alabaster jackpot.
A sluggish, backwards-compatible zodiac wheel.

The Smoking Typewriter

A paper tiger burning bright,
in the typewriter of the night.
Is it a romantic or a stalker
who worships at that metal altar?

In what distant ages dead and gone
lurk those balladeers, typing on?
Crescendos from midnight till dawn,
criss-crossed keys clacking as they yawn?

Ancient slack-jawed bards have ever,
to ting of carriage bell and whirr of lever,
tapped out peewee squibs that sputter,
and then flare out as love-lorn mutter.

With fangs of white-out and stripy smears,
as carbon copy from the roller tears:
a paper tiger burning bright,
in savage typewriter of the night.

Qwertyuiop! Qwertyuiop!

Jamie Oliver's TV Dinner

How can I cook thee? Let me count the ways.
You've been tubbed, you've been rubbed, you've been scrubbed.
You're lovable, huggable and eatable. Get out the pots and pans.
I peels an onion; I defrosts a chook; I chops, therefore I hams.
Gather round for a TV natter. I just want to say cheese whizz.
Not Gordon Ramsay's pan-sizzled bull's pizzle,
nor Nigella Lawson's rum-soaked strawberry tart;
thumping beefcake, groaning cheesecake, reek of artichoke heart.
Lovely-jubbly, smile sugar-coated, rosy as a cherub's posterior;
bunch of carrots in one hand, bunch of rhubarb in the other.
Ritzy nosh-up with high-end bubbly, breast of roasted pigeon—
pile high the platter till the pukka tucker teeter-totters;
only remember, never eat anything bigger than your head;
never eat anything prettier than you are.
Never eat anything that just walked in and sat down in the kitchen.

The People-Smuggler's Beard

There was the Brother Baxter louse-bearing beard.
Karl Stead wore a turtleneck with a beard.
How many sprouting potato-eyes to make
Sebastian Black's great beard of the 1970s?
The hog-riding bikie's beard, red as summer rātā;
the rash beard; the spurious sporran;
the short beard, springy as gutta-percha.
Tartan beards of lairds; bed-cover beards;
tūī lurking in bird's-nest beards with twigs,
to chorus a bush creed for greenies.

They were the oracles of their day,
the elders who pursed their lips,
and shook their heads and faded away,
gnawing fingernails and stroking jihadist beards.
Moses, patriarch of the longhairs,
ringletted Nebuchadnezzar, Karl Marx
and his jeroboam of beard, the unshaven Shavians.
Walt Whitman's salt-and-pepper bardic chops.
Ned Kelly's stringybark face-fungus brought him down,
the false beard of Ezra Pound,
the chin fluff of incipient beardies waits to be found.
Allen Ginsberg's pubic beard in the shape of the USA,
hiding a bomb or a bicycle or a B-52,
crossing the border at Mexicali;
Allen Ginsberg, alone, naked,
with knapsack, watch, camera, poem, and beard.

Plaited, pig-tailed, weedwhacking wonders;
Dundreary whiskers combed into a hairshirt.
The prickling wisp; the curly-wurly convoluted;

the spurred and booted; the deeply rooted.
The straight Ho Chi Minh trail beard;
the Gilbert and Sullivan vaudevillian beard;
the Jerusalem syndrome redeemer's beard;
the Stockholm syndrome kidnapper's beard;
the cybercaliphate's beheaded beard.
Beards with cobwebs and rigging and cordage.
The beard in its cups, making a tingle in nostrils,
that yabba-yabba, woof-woof gurgle-beard—
because Bacchus has drowned more men than Neptune.
The desperate beard, the daily beard, the beard that disappeared.

Poem for Ben Brown

Hey Ben, no matter how you jive,
you'll never get out of this poem alive.
Like Diamond Lil and D'Arcy Cresswell, Carmen Rupe,
and Uncle Scrim, and the Rawleigh's Man—
have you heard of him?—
you'll never get out of this poem alive.
You push the pedals, I'll steer, we'll both drive,
but you'll never get out of this poem alive.
Like Amy Bock's Petticoat Pioneers, Godfrey Bowen's
Click Go the Shears, Dame Ngaio Marsh's
murdering musterers;
like Canon Bob Lowe, and Tommy-boy Adderley,
Monte Holcroft, and Minnie Dean,
you'll never get out of this poem alive.
You can hula-hoop all the way to the top
of the Beehive,
but you'll never get out of this poem alive.
Like Ron Jorgensen's disappearance,
Mr Asia's debt clearance,
Phil Warren's firebombed nightclub entrance,
you'll never get out of this poem alive.
Never get out, never get out,
no matter how much you jump and shout.
Them's the breaks, them's ain't fakes,
them's knowing what it takes.
Like a roll-call of lucky beasts,
or New Zealand's surfing greats, WB Sutch,
Mickey Savage, Prince Tui Teka, Lofty Blomfield,
John A Lee or JKB—
I speak on behalf of the nation,
so please refrain from expectoration—

you'll never ever get out of this poem alive.
Bruno Lawrence, Rewi Alley, Hector Bolitho,
and my Aunt Sally, Selwyn Toogood, Mack Herewini,
Possum Bourne, and Chew Chong—
they never got out of this poem alive.
Like Mother Mary Aubert, the Man Alone,
the Woman at the Store, Miss Eileen Duggan's
worsted plain, Charles Kingsford Smith's balsa
tri-plane—never get out, never get out.
Bruce Mason's fruity tones, Patricia Bartlett's groans,
Lew Pryme didn't make old bones;
the surrealistic pillow of Philip Clairmont,
the deary-me of Beatrice Tinsley,
the what's all this then of Truby King
the never mind all that of Sir Wally Nash.
Let's agree, to a degree—
you'll never get out, never get out,
never get out of this poem alive!

Obelisk

By the stone tower of the Anzac obelisk,
larks are ascending and walnuts descending.
Golden morning was juicy as a Packham pear,
now autumn's evening sifts its dry yellow light,
and time's gold gilt comes off in my hands.
Harping on, wasps string a lyre through gardens.
Flocks are airborne; whales spout on the horizon.
Seasons sow, ripen, harvest, and are barren.
Whiffs of river slime drift from rock snot,
and a green phosphorescent mould grows
all over my clammy, sticky fingers.
Snails' trails are all across leopard-print lawns.
The scratchy twigs quibble with birdsong.
The hunted rook staggers from tree to tree.
Rag-winged leaves blow from stark branches.
The angry, half-inched leaf mulch
gets up and totters away, buzzing.
A mountain's cracked cauldron steams.
Somewhere north, a chuckling creek
drowns the rain-gauge
and fleeces float to the waiting sea.

My Inner Aotearoa

My inner Aotearoa is smoky blue gums
in a corner of the khaki paddock,
a crunching noise underfoot from withered grasses,
                    the tarred road bleeding in the sun,
                    creek beds shoaling as a dusty river,
                    bush decked with trails of clematis flowers.
When I only had gorse in my pockets,
I went in fear of the spiralling arms
of Crab Nebula, somewhere overhead.
Now I escape to stamp the black bubbles
of hot bitumen as if treading grapes,
and run headlong up Breakneck Road.

My inner Aotearoa is a need to brake
to descend the incline,
and I want it steep, steeper, steepest.
                    A riddled leaf smites my wet cheek,
                    a hailstorm of lies
                    is illuminated in a lightning flash.
A glacier shrinks to the size of an ice-cube,
to be crunched, steadily.
But dig deep, deeper, deepest,
throw up topsoil till it rains sustenance.
The magnitude of the extra grunt
resounds, as one more raindrop falls.

My inner Aotearoa is a lake's rise
and fall, land's a heartbeat.
The transcendental meaning of flesh
is raised on a bier,
                    on a balsawood cross,
                    on a barbecue grill,
                    on a hospital bed.
Light thickens and sours in the milk bottle,
glugs heavily in the sinkhole,
leading to the place where all sinkholes empty.
So just hold your nose and jump,
into eternal darkness made visible.

Thirty Days of Night

Night, as the last amber drains from heaven.
Night, as I dip my quill into a dark pool and begin.
Night, as an earthquake trembles a chandelier.
Night's coal hulks rotting at anchor.
Night's coal heaver,
glow-wormy, tattooed with blue light.
Night's Bible, leather-black
and gold-tooled, on the table.
Night, little worms of flame
shooting through blackening pages.
Night beyond the black sump,
the wallow, all the yackety-yak.
Night's trouble of fools,
watching while the colour of night rages.
Some new-fangled thing or other,
made of fire and night.

Night over crosses in cemeteries,
over glimmers of hospitals, auto-wreckers' yards.
Night's fingers that tap the steering wheel.
Night's zoo beasts that nag neighbourhoods.
Night's siren, as if a rabid banshee
has gone off-slope to echolocate down a canyon.
Night hiding the secrets of the chic
in their thready suits.
Night, removing sock-shod feet
from yawning shoes.
Night, and those awful black briefs.
Night, alive and tarry, and entering on tippy-toes.
Night knows what it wants,
it wants nocturnes fried in grease.

Night that grabs you by the lapels
at the edge of the abyss.

Night's chiaroscuro crumbled to charcoal.
Night, and the black gorge flash-floods,
to sluice across tapu ground.
Night, where the express doesn't stop.
Night, a stab in the dark,
under the Dog Star.
Night, a lonely shout into the thunder.
Night that archives itself in stealth
inside the history of shadows.
Night that weighs its grams, grain by grain,
out in a golden balance.
Night, as if a nameless rogue, a fugue,
as if no, nil, nix, not, never.
Night bells for the dying and the risen again.
As mica glitters in schist, so hoar frost night.

The Great Wave

There is no god but God, go mongooses in the monsoon.
The rains thrum on empty biscuit tin drums
to rattle Suva market and flick your face.
The jail's walls are ivory; a rainbow crooks an elbow.
The old shoeshine boy begs for money
for a cup of tea and two pieces of bread.
Everybody wears jogging shoes and sneakers,
the jingle-jangle of the bangle-seller is drowned
by a radio that could walk five hundred miles,
and then go walking on the moon to a bass line by Sting.
A crimson hibiscus lei drapes the punchbowl
at the bar, where I renovate my inner temple
and wait for the night to extend my winning streak,
as hotel staff slice tops off fresh pineapples
to reach garlanded pinnacles of mirrors.
A hinge bends to lift a drift log from the surf.
Thus spake Zarathustra to the fa`afafine:
bruise me with purple shadows of evening fallen
over searched caves of eyes that lids close on.
I listen to the ocean chant words from Rotuma.
The *Mariposa* is a butterfly between islands.
A heatwave, fathoms green, whose light spreads
its coconut oil or ghee or thick candlenut soot,
twinkles like fireflies over plantation gloom,
and heart's surge is the world's deep breath.
I learn to love every move the great wave makes;
it coils you into each silken twist of foam,
blown far, all the way to salt-touched Tonga,
with mango pits, wooden baler, shells awash.
My uncle, swimming from New Zealand, wades
out of the sea and wades on shore at Levuka,

where my grandmother is staring out
from her hillside grove of trees waiting for him.

Men's Group

He's a marooned kingpin
inside a circle of empty chairs,
ripping away the silver lining.

He has risen shriven
from his wicked ways,
a freedom camper unbound.

He has a watching crowd of disbelievers.
He hiccups his way
through a recital of misfortune.

He has the unction of an undertaker.
He takes the measure of warmth
to be found in a shot glass.

He wears a number of competing deodorants,
and his head has the glossy sheen
of a recently polished doorknob.

He's the mute witness.
He's been consuming up large since forever.
He grubs the same ground over.

His language is lickerish, bootylicious.
He raises a cloud of insects,
and is admired by a tūī, a tomtit and a rifleman.

He fudges whether he has ever served in the SAS.
He is absolutely sweet and choice,
and off to bro' repairs.

Scale

Jump from pram, push-chair, with excitement,
leap off springboard, vault in gymnasium—
chase along, surge forwards, running strong.

If you see something rising, then help it rise,
shinny up a ladder, handhold, foothold,
climb through branches, level after level.

Start from a standstill; be bold in movement,
glad dreamer at dawn, stepper on a treadmill,
the stair-dancer soaring on to the next floor.

Strike out for peaks, vaulting ascender,
steady at the heels of advancing figures,
tramping before you in formal procession,

to balconies of cloud above the high lakes.
Go where creeks tumble, distant birds spiral,
as gravity's drag starts to rake you earthwards.

Ascend over years, to cliffs and steep precipice,
to slips and stumbles, an ever-narrowing path,
then slowly up the mountain in closing mist.

NEW POEMS (2020)

Almost Once

Almost once,
timber combusted then flared;
hot coal spent,
the burnt stick bent its head.

Almost once,
each match charred
in matchbox smoulder;
more dead matches, one red soldier.

Almost once,
brands began to burn;
out jumped the devil,
with endless supplies of gunpowder.

Almost once,
stones struck sparks
for revels of light,
that danced in scarlet and black.

Almost once,
a nimbus vanished,
melted to charcoal and tar;
darkness harvested fire.

Almost once,
a book of maxims lit
with hellish glow,
scorching fingertips.

Almost once,
flames flashed from paper,
fanned to a blaze, whirled as ash,
then sank as a handful of grit.

Two Mosques, Christchurch

The poem writes the gunman invisible:
a him who hates so much is indefensible.
Scrupulous, they followed their beliefs to peace
he chose to deny and scythe with brutal lies.
Their blood unfurls as that of martyrs,
though they never wanted their altars.
All that's impure, he brought with a smirk;
he will be forever cobwebbed by the dark,
his darkness sawn out of rocks in his head.
But they will bloom forever, each one dead,
as the nation mourns and mountains crack.
Sad days amid rainbow petals, freshened stems,
a tide of grief that will never leave the path,
that winds with so many threads and colours.
He wanted ammunition; they bade him welcome.
He wanted crime; they gave him forgiveness.
He wanted erasure to fill the hole in his soul.
They barely sought to acknowledge him at all,
but only as a shooter who rose in a jabber,
and blind with loathing pulled the trigger.
Let them be a mass of flowers,
       that are vessels of keening spirits.
Let them be a mass of flowers,
       bunched and wrinkled and handwritten.
Let them be a mass of flowers,
       like the remains of a maze trampled down.
Let them be a mass of flowers,
       like a storm system stirring the ground.
Let them be a mass of flowers,
       like a compass and a journey.
Let them be a mass of flowers,

that winds from mosque to mosque,
and then around the city, dusted with pollen and history.

The Burning Cathedral

The nave of the church hangs suspended in gloom,
tall as the ghost of Charles de Gaulle,
who is Charlie Hebdo walking backwards for Christians;
and nuns in black habits cluster in consternation
to gaze at big-clawed toes of hounds of hellfire;
and the spire of Notre-Dame is scorched to cinders
and gone for a burton, like the Last Will and Testament
of the vagabond poet François Villon.
Paris sparrows, like shrunken velociraptors, hop
to peck at the brittle, onion-soup stones of Notre-Dame;
they fly like gnomes at those bones that make hollow groans;
as kickflip flâneurs, and parkour postmoderns,
and rock climbers with rubber slippers and chalky digits
flexing to climb the titanic bulk going under,
shout: this cathedral's on fire, blazing in the night,
blaze on Notre-Dame, when you've gone we'll start a dope farm.
An archangel catches a desecration of tourists
in the spotlight of his fixated beam,
he's taking the pith, and his marble teeth are green;
and a media chorus of commentary pours forth,
and the faithful are ordering jigsaw puzzles online,
to offer up a personal rebuild of the Cathedral of Notre-Dame,
in the manner of Buddhist rebirth or the architecture of Islam.
X-rays reveal the massive carcass of an ancient
beast, cobbled together like Frankenstein's monster,
with famine, starvation, blood, mortar, Les Misérables.
A fog of black soot drifts through Left Bank twilight,
Jean-Paul Sartre's selling existentialism to billionaires:
white ash sifts down, all that smoke gone up as prayers.
What God hath wrought raises the Pope's eyebrows,
and Jesus hangs on the cross with the skinny thighs

of a weightwatcher who has completed the programme.
And Napoléon B on his knees, eager to be Emperor,
crowns himself impatiently in the church of Notre-Dame.
And Quasimodo with Esméralda over his shoulder
is doing rope tricks in the bell-tower of Notre-Dame.
De Sade and Marie Antoinette bound on the gallows cart.
Grotesques, banshees, demons, all the chimeras,
chewing on stone chickens and pâté de foie gras.
Birds of ill-omen roosting amongst neo-Nazis
whose inflammable remains have seen off the flames,
as beggars wrapped in cardboard blankets lie
on the banks of the Seine like broken saints,
fallen from the empty niches of Notre-Dame.
With nose extruded like the Concorde
leaving Paris for New York, Macron
looks heavenward for answers on the steps of Notre-Dame;
and Paris hives of yellowjackets buzz and sing,
huzzah huzzah at so much bloody chutzpah.
So we will remember the processions of sinners
and their echoes in the greater silence of Notre-Dame,
while the planet goes on turning, the planet we've set burning
to suck up all the oxygen in the room.
Centuries of burn baby burn, and unholy gusts of flame,
as gargoyles spew acid rain down the façade of Notre-Dame.

Bubble Life

Bond bubble,
housing bubble,
tech bubble,
emerging markets bubble.
Escapist bubble,
hubble bubble,
difficult bubble,
future bubble.
Bubble, bubble,
toil and trouble,
a bubble to bamboozle,
a bubble to befuddle.
Outlaw bubble,
dodgeball bubble,
pimp my hog bubble,
rock star bubble.
Libertarian bubble,
green bubble,
ninety-year-old bubble,
empty bubble.
A bubble to buckle on
like castle armour,
a bubble to tackle from
and leap shovel-ready from.
A bubble to hold forth
hands coated with sanitiser,
barricaded behind
big bales of toilet paper.
A bubble for the foreseeable,
a personal digital archivisation bubble,
a dysfunctional bubble,

a chuckle bubble.
Put a candle in the window bubble,
constant smell of home-baking bubble,
view from Madame Tussaud's basement Zoom bubble,
boodle boodle boodle bubble.
Over each supersensible soap bubble,
to stay safe from a disease that haunts
the world's best minds and taunts
with its stealthy lassoes of spittle—
an iridescent bubble of hope floats.

President Fillgrave

President Fillgrave going full confrontal,
with his twisted lame stabbing finger of blame,
and his sidekick Glumdaclitch Mitch,
and the trumpeting elephantine bulk
of the Republican sulk, clinging on.
Death rides a white golf cart,
wearing its invariable smiley orange face,
despite the grey of the crowd.
President Fillgrave, the busted orange flush,
with his fund of slush, his dirty hush-hush,
his strung-out husky poison potion of verbal mush.
Bunkered down with Covid on the brain,
sheltering in place with the virus,
listening to 'Wrecking Ball' by Miley Cyrus,
ticking off on his meretricious Christmas wish list,
the last weird wizard battle of the West,
pinnacled dim in the intense inane.
President Fillgrave, he don't give a damn, 'cos he's Uncle Sham,
he's married to the Mob, he's a made guy,
he owes them his little pinkie,
if not the whole of his tiny hands.
President Fillgrave,
he left his stone-cold heart in Frisco,
he left his bone spurs in Texas,
he left his pearly white teeth sunk in the rump
of some very fine people,
he left the ankles of the Statue of Liberty
tied to an anchor and thrown in the Hudson River,
he left his collection of empty bleach bottles
to the Presidential Library.
President Fillgrave.

The Umbrella Movement

Hymn book umbrella, march forward umbrella,
flap open umbrella, catch breeze umbrella,
blown backwards umbrella, busted ribs umbrella,
mourner black umbrella, yellow sun umbrella,
turning wheel umbrella, flying home umbrella.

Umbrellas hosed away by the water cannon,
umbrellas that push the envelope of commentary,
umbrella ideogram, umbrella lightning rod,
seize the handle, press the lever, raise it high,
into frontline barricades and pepper spray.

Crumple brella, tumble brella, humble brella,
jumble brella, killer brella, pum-pum brella,
quick umbrella, wonder brella, dreck brella.

Must dash, but what a splash, ripped fabric sails on,
good golly, my brolly has taken on a life of its own,
and joined a great shelter of umbrellas, dancing
                        like a Chinese dragon.

Len Lye's Wind Wand

Bendy baton, swizzle stick, swagger stick parade,
a pole vaulter's pole catapulted skyward,
performing spells at breezy dawn;
a spiral inside a clear glass marble,
a twister bearing the bob of a marker buoy.
Within its moist fog coat, the mountain is coy,
the bee rides the daisy flower back and forth.
Tall wand, a dowser's twitcher, down to earth,
curves to the gusts, inclines to the view,
floats with sphere, a bubble on air;
and then conducts an auction tender
between the mountain and the silver sea,
forest and bird, flax and river,
town and country, wave and whisper,
mountain white as Te Whiti's albatross feather.

The Letter Zed

From zealot to ziggurat,
that zeitgeist, that zoetrope
is Zealandia, son,
wear it on your lapel for your mother's sake.
Zugzwang ran the zoo,
and the zoo was an ark
for Zealandia and all who thrived there,
at the end of the alphabet,
knowing they were lucky last,
possessing the Anzac spirit and abundant lemon zest.
Even zambucks carrying a concussed player
zonked from the paddock,
zigzagged to the ambulance.
Those in Zephyrs and Zodiacs
bound down State Highway 1,
heading home on a metal throne with rubber
tyres, knew they sat at the zenith.
Their zipped-up zippers shone,
their ziffs purred with satisfaction,
Zespri was their favourite sorbet.
Zowie! they went, zooming along,
catch the zeds from those over there.
We're zippy, but they are just zizz,
just z-listers in zombie droves.
Thataway, zanies chill, out of zone,
singing zip-a-dee-aye, zip-a-dee-eh,
zip-a-dee-doo-dah day, to zydeco.
They make zippo or zilch gestures,
they launch zingers from a phone,
each a zillionaire living on pure air,
till zapped by the self-same bug-zapper

that one day will zap
Zealandia back to zero.

David Eggleton reads at the WORD Christchurch Spring Festival 2020.
Photograph by John Allison

Notes and Acknowledgements

'Almost Once' is an ekphrastic poem, responding to Brett Whiteley's 1991 sculpture *Almost Once*, also known as 'The Big Matchsticks', located in the domain beside the Art Gallery of New South Wales in Sydney.

'Len Lye's Wind Wand' is another ekphrastic poem, responding to Len Lye's 1999 kinetic sculpture *The Wind Wand*, located on the waterfront near the centre of New Plymouth.

I have in places revised, changed or updated some previously published poems, mostly with the spelling of words in te reo Māori. On a few occasions I have made minor word changes and adjustments to phrasing or line measures in the interests of clarity or euphony, while keeping faith with the style and intent of the earlier versions.

I wish to acknowledge the publishers of my previous collections from which these poems have been selected: Penguin Books New Zealand, Auckland University Press, Otago University Press and Otakou Press.

My thanks to the team at Otago University Press for their mahi in preparing this selection of poems for publication: Rachel Scott, Vanessa Manhire, Imogen Coxhead and Fiona Moffat. I would also like to thank Anna Hodge for her editorial eye and wise counsel on matters of poetic style. And I thank artist Nigel Brown for agreeing to contribute artwork and helping develop the cover design.

Special thanks to Fieke Neuman for her endless support. I also must acknowledge my immediate fanau: Frank, Glen, Tonu-Shane, Brenda, Talei and Koa. Above all, thanks in memoriam to my extraordinary parents, an attraction of opposites. Noa`ia e mauri. Arohanui.